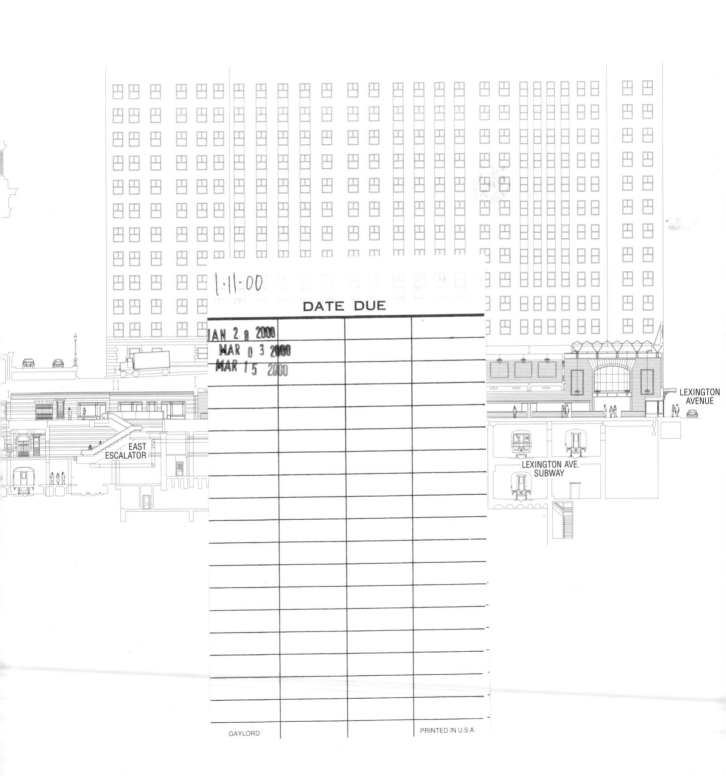

DATE DUE

EAST
ESCALATOR

LEXINGTON
AVENUE

LEXINGTON AVE.
SUBWAY

GAYLORD   PRINTED IN U.S.A.

GRAND CENTRAL

GRAND CENTRAL

GATEWAY
TO A MILLION LIVES

JOHN BELLE

MAXINNE R. LEIGHTON

W. W. NORTON & COMPANY
NEW YORK LONDON

The publication of this book was made possible in part by the generous support of *Furthermore*, the publication program of the J. M. Kaplan Fund.

Excerpt from Edgar Tafel, *About Wright* (New York: John Wiley & Sons, Inc., 1995), © 1995. Reprinted by permission of John Wiley & Sons, Inc. Cornel West quotation used courtesy of the author.

Excerpt on page 211 from "The Sky Line: Now Arriving" originally published in *The New Yorker*. Reprinted by permission.

We have made every attempt to credit sources and contact the appropriate parties. If there are any corrections needed, please contact W. W. Norton and proper changes will be made.

Design and typesetting in Adobe Garamond by Katy Homans with Jackie Goldberg

Library of Congress Cataloging-in-Publication Data

Belle, John.
Grand Central : gateway to a million lives / John Belle and Maxinne R. Leighton
p. cm.
Includes bibliographical references (p. 214–220) and index.
ISBN 0-393-04765-2
1. Grand Central Terminal (New York, N.Y.) 2. Warren & Wetmore—Criticism and interpretation. 3. Railroad stations—New York (State)—New York—Conservation and restoration. 4. New York (N.Y.)—Buildings, structures, etc.—Conservation and restoration. I. Leighton, Maxinne Rhea. II. Title.
NA6313.N4B45 1999
725'.31'097471—dc21
98-51419

CIP

W. W. Norton & Company, Inc., 500 Fifth Avenue, New York, N.Y. 10110
www.wwnorton.com

W. W. Norton & Company Ltd., 10 Coptic Street, London WC1A 1PU

1 2 3 4 5 6 7 8 9 0

CONTENTS

GRAND CENTRAL
TERMINAL

FOREWORD

Grand Central Terminal, originally built as a symbol of the Vanderbilts' personal fame and fortune, quickly became a building that passed literally and symbolically from their hands into the lives of the millions of daily users who made it their own. And, it was ordinary citizens who ultimately formed the constituency that saved it from destruction. The grassroots preservation movement made its stand at Grand Central; it was their Alamo. Consequently, securing Grand Central's continued existence has compelled architects to rethink their role in protecting our built heritage. Grand Central is a cathedral for every man and woman; its arresting public space has touched the hearts and remained in the memories of the millions who have passed through its doors.

For the authors of this book, Grand Central is a place where the language of civic architecture and the celebration of individual lives coexist in one great building. For John Belle, the architect for the restoration and a founding partner of Beyer Blinder Belle, Grand Central is the holy grail of the landmarks preservation movement. For Maxinne Leighton, an associate partner of the firm, the joys and travails of the human spirit have seeped into its very walls. For both, it is the heartbeat of New York.

When our firm was put in charge of this restoration we felt a guardianship and a personal responsibility for its rebirth. As the architect for the restoration, every detail became a personal obsession, the design of the new east staircase a personal crusade. The client and the public had given their unflinching support to the plans for the restoration of the Terminal, and it was our job not to fail them. For each of us, having shared a unique involvement in the building's rebirth over a span of ten years, telling the story of Grand Central became more than just a historical or a literal account; it became a personal one. This remarkable building showed how it can get inside our being and completely take over our lives.

The restoration is now complete. We have handed the building back to its users in renewed glory. But readers should keep in mind that Grand Central's future existence and contribution to our civic life is dependent on their continued guardianship, for in the truest sense it will remain the best of public spaces only if we watch over it as zealously as we fought to save and restore it.

Grand Central's limestone mass is punctuated by decorative lights along the Vanderbilt Avenue sidewalk.

© Peter Aaron/Esto

GRAND CENTRAL

GATEWAY TO A MILLION LIVES

CHAPTER ONE

SAVING AN ARCHETYPE

Is it not cruel to let our city die by degrees, stripped of all her proud monuments, until there will be nothing left of all her history and beauty to inspire our children? If they are not inspired by the past of our city, where will they find the strength to fight for her future?
—JACQUELINE KENNEDY ONASSIS

Grand Central, one of the greatest railroad terminals of all time, was first and foremost a space created for people. With its high ceilings and open spaces; sunlight dramatically filtering through its windows; warm, muted tones; creamy, sensual marble floors and blue-green heavens above, this splendid gateway became a space where millions of lives crossed and touched one another on their way to somewhere else. Its enduring presence has worked itself into our hearts, becoming deeply entrenched in the cultural fabric of our city and our country.

The threat of the destruction of Grand Central Terminal not only challenged the life of a loved and cherished building but also brought into question our society's values. Were we a society that would allow motivation for profit to succeed at the expense of history and tradition? If shared history binds a city of strangers together through a neighborhood or a single building, do we not have a responsibility to protect that? Is New York a city without a soul?

The fight to save Grand Central was a turning point in how Americans value their architecture and the responsibility of historic preservation in protecting the legacies of society. "Great civilizations of the past recognized that their citizens had aesthetic needs, that great architecture gave nobility and respite to their daily lives," wrote Jacqueline Kennedy Onassis. "They built fine buildings, spacious parks, beautiful markets. Their places of assembly, worship, ceremony, or arrival and departure were not merely functional but spoke to the dignity of man." This statement was representative of the attitude of those organizing to preserve Grand Central from destruction and whose outcries eventually led to the 1978 decision by the U.S. Supreme Court to uphold the landmark status of Grand Central Terminal.

With the New York Central Building in the distance and surrounding sites having been developed (as conceived in the original Terminal City plan), Grand Central's southern facade acts as a triumphal gateway to the city. (Photograph circa 1930.)

Courtesy of MTA/Metro-North Collection

The story of Grand Central's survival began in the 1950s, when voices for development were becoming very aggressive. After World War II, people looked confidently toward their future. The desire to leave the past behind became pervasive in American culture; as a result, much of our existing built environment was destroyed. As this point of view spread, few historic landmark buildings remained unthreatened. Even Grand Central was vulnerable. Its railroad owners wanted to tear it down and replace it with what they considered the symbol of contemporary American spirit: the skyscraper. Numerous skyscraper plans were put forth by some of the most renowned architects of the time.

In 1954, Robert Young, chairman of the board of the New York Central Railroad with William Zeckendorf, president of Webb & Knapp, a real estate development company, proposed I. M. Pei's "Hyperboloid," a creative, innovative, steel, geometric, 108-story wonder that was as visually daunting as its nomenclature. Proposed to replace the existing Grand Central Terminal, it would have been the world's tallest building—unseating the Empire State Building—and at 4.8 million square feet, the largest commercial office space in the world.

Patrick McGinnis, president of the New York, New Haven and Hartford Railroad (joint owners of Grand Central Terminal with New York Central), proposed a different scheme: a 55-story office building designed by Fellheimer and Wagner, with a heliport, 2,400-car garage, restaurants, and retail to keep as many as possible of the 30,000 office workers away from the East Side midday pedestrian traffic jam. The proposal also included extensive changes to the street patterns, including rebuilding the curving Park Avenue overpass into a straight line. Fellheimer and Wagner was the successor firm to Reed & Stem, one of the two firms responsible for the original design of Grand Central. Ironically, Fellheimer and Wagner's office tower would have destroyed not only a part of society's past but also Fellheimer's own personal heritage, for Fellheimer himself had worked on the design of the Terminal building fifty-one years earlier, at the beginning of his career.

These schemes brought into question publicly whether a monument should be destroyed if its owner's tax and revenue problems demanded it. *Architectural Forum*, one of the leading architectural magazines of its day,

A model of I. M. Pei's 1954 "Hyperboloid," a 108-story office structure that would have replaced the Terminal.

Courtesy of Pei Cobb Freed & Partners

In 1958, Emery Roth & Sons designed Grand Central City, the initial proposal that evolved into the Pan Am Building in 1963.

Courtesy of Emery Roth & Sons, drawing by Robert Schwartz

thought not and led a crusade to save Grand Central. Approximately 235 architects from all over the United States sent letters through *Architectural Forum* to Young and McGinnis with pleas to save the Terminal's Main Concourse.

Over the years, Grand Central's Main Concourse had become a kind of public assembly room for the people of New York City. In 1923 a memorial service was held for President Harding; 30,000 people gathered there to hear President Truman deliver a speech in 1952; and a weekly radio drama in the 1940s and 1950s called *Grand Central Station* came into the homes of people nationally, endearing Grand Central and its Main Concourse to them.

"It is rumored that you and the directors contemplate pulling down the Grand Central Concourse," wrote an impassioned citizen in an appeal to the chairman of the New York Central Railroad.

"Please don't let it be said you had anything to do with such a sacrilege. Surely you must realize what it means to New Yorkers, to the nation, and to most persons who have had to or must pass through your great city. There are some things that money can't buy or replace. They have become a part of the people. Please, please don't touch it." Other letters followed in what quickly became an open debate about Grand Central's future.

After World War II long-distance train travel declined, automobile and airline travel became symbolic of America moving forward into a new era. Based on its continued loss of income, the New York Central Railroad concluded that Grand Central was no longer viable as a railroad terminal and should be replaced with modern office buildings. "We carefully weighed our own pride in the present building," wrote Alfred Fellheimer, in defense of his skyscraper replacing Grand Central, "and its emotional and esthetic significance to people all over the world. Our reluctant but firm conclusion is that neither pride nor reverence should be permitted to clot the vitality of a great metropolis. In turn, that very vitality may guarantee that if one expression of human aspirations must be destroyed in the process of growth, it will be replaced by an even

greater one." Alfred E. Perlman, chief executive officer of the New York Central Railroad, unable to achieve a consensus about the building and bring one of the two skyscraper schemes to fruition, threatened to end all commuter service into Grand Central and abandon the Terminal completely unless Mayor Robert Wagner and the State of New York helped him deal with overcoming his company's losses.

As the debate continued, the two railroad magnates Young and McGinnis decided to join forces in Grand Central's development. They agreed to continue working with the developer Erwin Wolfson, who had proposed Fellheimer and Wagner's scheme initially. Known as a promoter, contrac-

In January 1961, the Terminal's six-story office and baggage building was demolished to become the site of the Pan Am Building.
Corbis/Bettmann ©

tor, and building owner, Wolfson was quick to identify failure and make whatever changes were necessary to win. He abandoned Fellheimer and Wagner's scheme and in 1958 hired Emery Roth & Sons to design Grand Central City: a complex of buildings that would not necessitate the destruction of the Terminal. Not satisfied with Roth's design, Wolfson added Walter Gropius and Pietro Belluschi to the team. This collaborative design, initially proposed February 18, 1959, as Grand Central City, was completed in 1963 as the 59-story, 2.4 million square foot Pan Am Building (known today as the MetLife Building). Erected on a three-acre site immediately north of the Terminal building, it was built on the site of the six-story Grand Central office and baggage building located above the tracks. The great interior of Grand Central Terminal remained intact, not because of any design conviction or public pressure but because James O. Bolisi, vice president of real estate for New York Central failed to include the Terminal building in the air-rights package awarded to Wolfson for development.

Though the Concourse was saved, the once dramatic Park Avenue vista framed by the three arched windows of the Terminal and the delicate Grand

Central Tower behind was gone. Instead of space and sky, an aggressive 59-story tower shaped like an elongated octagon, encased in metal, concrete, and glass, loomed over the Terminal. The threat to Grand Central's survival came from proposals for what was to be built around her and on top of her.

But despite all this, nothing threatened the continued existence of the building more than what was happening at New York's other classically beautiful gateway: Pennsylvania Railroad Station. Designed by McKim, Mead & White, this nine-acre site composed of travertine and granite, 84 Doric columns, and a vaulted concourse was breathless in its monumentality. Completed three years earlier than Grand Central Terminal, Penn Station was designed to be the symbol of the Pennsylvania Railroad's successful competition with the New York Central. And though it had become one of New York's most important public spaces, by the 1960s, with railroads in decline and its physical appearance waning, Penn Station was in the way of real estate profit and development.

The Pennsylvania Railroad's plan to demolish Penn Station was made public in 1960. Its successor was a cramped and architecturally bland station, topped by what the *New York Times* described as a "futuristic sports palace [known today as Madison Square Garden] with a 33-story skyscraper." And though many asked why it wasn't possible to build without destroying the best of our past, it wasn't until 1962 that AGBANY, the Action Group for Better Architecture in New York, was formed by Jordan Gruzen, Norman Jaffe, Diana Kirsch, Peter Samton, Norval White, and Elliot Willensky to fight the plans to replace Penn Station with Madison Square Garden. AGBANY held a rally of over 200 architects on August 2, 1962, which was reported in *Architectural Forum* as "a few hundred militant people standing in the way of a much needed sports complex." It was too little, too late. Mayor Wagner dismissed AGBANY's pleas, petitions, and demonstrations. The city planning commission under Wagner's leadership had allowed the special permit and thus enabled the Madison Square Garden Corporation to destroy Penn Station. In 1962 the mayor appointed a study commission to draft a landmarks law.

In August 1963, the day the demolition began, six architects wore black armbands and carried signs that read "Shame." For the first time it became clear

The 59-story Pan Am Building (Emery Roth & Sons, Pietro Belluschi, and Walter Gropius, architects), overwhelms the Terminal and shuts off the Park Avenue vista.

Courtesy of MTA/Metro-North Collection

On August 2, 1962, AGBANY (Action Group for Better Architecture in New York) held a rally outside Penn Station to protest its scheduled demolition. Among the 200 participants are (from left to right) Ulrich Franzen, Peter Samton, Aline Saarinen, Philip Johnson, and Mrs. Bliss Parkinson.
David Hirsch, photographer. Courtesy of Peter Samton.

Pennsylvania Station's lofty spaces of Roman scale are demolished piece by piece as the new steel for Madison Square Garden rises through the floor.
Collection of The New-York Historical Society

that, without any government agency as a voice on behalf of the city's monuments, all historic buildings were vulnerable to destruction. One of the counter workers in Penn Station's Saverin restaurant summed it up when he said, "This city's got the right name—New York. Nothing ever gets old around here."

Perhaps it was the double blow—the demolition of Penn Station together with the completion of the Pan Am Building—that gave the "save Grand Central" constituents their greatest scare. The realization grew that Grand Central could have a fate similar to Pennsylvania Station's. If the political climate of shunning the past prevailed and the great architectural monuments of previous eras continued to be destroyed, Grand Central would end as a pile of rubble in New Jersey's meadowlands.

The demolition of Penn Station continued into 1965. Although protests and demonstrations could not reverse the political decision to destroy Penn Station, civic protests continued to build a climate for establishing a public agency to safeguard the historic fabric of the city. On April 19, 1965, Mayor Wagner signed the New York City Landmarks Preservation Law, thereby establishing for the first time a mechanism for saving the city's architectural heritage. The law provided for the commission to have a membership consisting of at least three architects, a realtor, a city planner or landscape architect, an historian, and at least one resident from each of the five boroughs. Just a year after its formation, on May 10, 1966, the Landmarks Preservation Commission held a

public hearing on the proposed designation of Grand Central Terminal as a landmark. On August 2, 1967, after several public hearings, the eleven-member Landmarks Preservation Commission designated the exterior of Grand Central Terminal a landmark. Their reasoning was clear. Because of its special character, historical and aesthetic qualities, and value as part of New York's development, heritage, and cultural history, it must be protected. The Commission went on to cite that Grand Central, "one of the great buildings of America, evokes a spirit that is unique in the City. . . . Monumental in scale, this great building functions as well today as it did when built." The Board of Estimate, as provided by the Landmarks Law, confirmed the designation.

Though the Landmarks Preservation Commission's designation was a sheltering presence on paper, it was soon challenged. In February 1968, less than one year after the Landmarks Commission's designation of Grand Central, New York Central merged with the Pennsylvania Railroad and formed Penn Central. UGP Properties, Inc., with British developer Morris Saady at the helm, leased the air development rights over the terminal from Penn Central for fifty years. In 1903, William Wilgus coined the phrase "air rights." Originally, the use of air rights for surrounding development had made it economically feasible to create a building of this scale and grandeur. Ironically, now it was the same concept that threatened its destruction.

Enter Marcel Breuer, the distinguished architect of the Whitney Museum of American Art at Madison Avenue and 75th Street. Renowned internationally and greatly admired by his fellow architects, Breuer had an idea for a 55-story, 800-foot tower that would sit on top of Grand Central Terminal but would not totally destroy the building. Cantilevered over the roof of the terminal, it would integrate and retain part of the Main Concourse and the entire facade but would demolish the magnificent waiting room. This proposed building, named 175 Park Avenue, would be parallel to the Pan Am Building. Offering the railroad $1 million a year during construction and at least $3 million a year thereafter, UGP was determined to bring its business proposal to fruition.

In order to begin the proposed work, an application for a Certificate of No Exterior Effect was made to the Landmarks Preservation Commission by the Penn Central Company, UGP Properties, the New York and Harlem Railroad Company, and the 51st Street Realty Corporation. Since only the Beaux Arts exterior of the building had been landmarked and not the interior, there was no "legal" recourse to protect the waiting room or any part of the interior of the Main Concourse. There was some trepidation at Landmarks, and Harmon H. Goldstone, chairman of the Landmarks Preservation Commission, remembers one of his key people saying, "We can never stand up to this power; we're all going to have to knuckle under this one." To which Goldstone responded, "we may well be torpedoed, but let's go down with all flags flying."

On September 20, 1968, the Landmarks Preservation Commission rejected Breuer's initial proposal. A second application, this time for a certificate of appropriateness, together with an alternative proposal, was submitted on

In 1968 UGP Properties proposed a 55-story tower designed by Marcel Breuer. Two designs were prepared. Breuer I was cantilevered over the Terminal's roof; Breuer II Revised obliterated the exterior of the Terminal.

Marcel Breuer and Associates

January 20, 1969. Known as Breuer II, it obliterated the exterior of the terminal and restored the entire Main Concourse. Public hearings were set for three days in April with a decision from the commission by May. Concurrent with these hearings Penn Central and UGP Properties realized Breuer II was to be built on land that extended over a city-held easement that was outside the private developer's control. The Breuer II proposal was withdrawn and later resubmitted as Breuer II Revised, which was restricted to land controlled by UGP Properties. Public hearings were reopened in August 1969 on both Breuer I and Breuer II Revised.

The design of Breuer II Revised upped the ante. Not only was it three stories taller than Breuer I but it also required the demolition of much of the Terminal building; the Main Concourse, however, would be preserved and restored. The representatives of UGP argued that the concourse interior was the only part of the building worth saving, that the exterior had not been worth designating in the first place, and that it was the smarter choice to replace the current building with a good building by a famous architect than to risk, in the future, one being built by a lesser talent. Many in the architectural community supported Breuer's architectural design. The late Walter F. Wagner, Jr., editor of *Architectural Record*, said that the building would "make a powerful contribution to the overcrowded hub of New York City's transportation system." Peter Blake, in a Cityscape piece in *New York* magazine, shot down the critics of Breuer and Penn Central. "To sum up: there is no City Plan to which Breuer or anyone else could have conformed and so the 'villain' in this case is a City Planning Commission too spineless in the past to have fought for tough zoning laws and too unconcerned to have developed a master plan for the city as a whole. As for Penn Central, the 'villain' is not the Penn Central Railroad, but a society that permits and encourages wild and unrestricted speculation with the price of land."

The public hearings brought a strong showing for both sides of the issue. People who spoke in favor of the proposal included Murray Drabkin, UGP Properties, Inc.; Marcel Breuer and partner Herbert Beckhard; architect I. M. Pei; Roger Starr, representing the Citizens Housing and Planning Council; architect Edward Larrabee Barnes; Arthur Rosenblatt, administrator for architecture and planning at the Metropolitan Museum of Art; John Baur, director of the Whitney Museum; and other prominent New Yorkers.

Why so many well-respected professionals could have voted in favor of proposals that prophesied Grand Central's demise is indicative of a time in our history when people believed that preserving the old kept us trapped in the clutches of the past. "The prevailing image of preservationists," Harmon Goldstone said, "was of ladies in floppy hats and tennis shoes, joined by a few crackpots."

Those speaking against both proposals included then Congressman Edward Koch; Jean Paul Carlhian, representing the American Institute of Architects; Giorgio Cavaglieri, New York State Preservation Coordinator for the American Institute of Architects; Charles Hughes and Frederick Williams, representing the Municipal Art Society; Margo Gayle, representing the Victorian Society and the Village Neighborhood Committee; Architects David Todd and George Lewis, representing the New York Chapter of the American Institute of Architects, Professor James Marston Fitch of the School of Architecture at Columbia University (who later became the chairperson of historic preservation at Beyer Blinder Belle), and a roster of other prominent professionals. The vast majority of local and national architectural organizations spoke against the demolition or defacement of Grand Central, despite their respect for Breuer as one of their own.

While this was going on in New York, Marcel Breuer was receiving the American Institute of Architects' Gold Medal in Portland, Oregon, one of the most prestigious awards presented to an individual architect by his peers for a lifetime of work. During this award-winning but controversial time, Breuer adamantly stated that he would have refused a commission to design the Pan

Am Building and destroy the vistas that once existed, but that now with them gone he could accept the commission and produce the best possible design above Grand Central.

On August 26, 1969, Breuer I and Breuer II Revised were denied a Certificate of Appropriateness by the Landmarks Preservation Commission, and thus the developers were denied the right to build above Grand Central. " Is there any reason to destroy the great Terminal that we have because the Pan Am building is already there? Even though a less able architect than Breuer might produce a worse building," the Landmarks Preservation Commission wrote, "is that relevant to the City's landmark law? To have the exterior features of the building demolished is in violation of the landmark law. To protect a landmark, one does not tear it down. To perpetuate its architectural features, one does not strip them off. And that is just what the Breuer II Revised proposal would do."

The chairman of the City Planning Commission and a representative of the City Planning Department tried to solve the stalemate by offering Penn Central and the developer alternative sites to which they could transfer the unused development rights. It was an attempt by the city to help the developers get a return without destroying or impairing Grand Central. The Biltmore block on Vanderbilt Avenue between 43rd and 44th streets became the agreed-upon site to develop a 2.1 million square-foot office tower, of which 1.3 million square feet would constitute development rights transferred from Grand Central. The city had even gone so far as to change its zoning resolution in order to make this alternative scheme feasible. While this alternative was being negotiated, the country's economic health began to falter and New York City's real estate market went into a downturn. UGP/Penn Central decided it was not economically feasible to build at the Biltmore. With no new alternatives and unilateral rejection of their proposals by the Landmarks Commission there was only one option left: to let the courts decide.

The developers Saady and UGP together with Penn Central took the dispute from New York City's administrative jurisdiction and put it into the hands of the state courts. On October 7, 1969, they filed a lawsuit against the city in the Supreme Court of the State of New York—the lowest court in New York State's three-tiered system. They charged that the Landmarks Commission's refusal to approve any of their schemes was so financially burdensome that it amounted to an unconstitutional "taking" of their property without just compensation, and they claimed $8 million in lost earnings for every year the project was delayed. Was this, as they claimed, a violation of the Fifth and Fourteenth Amendments of the Constitution, which protect citizens from having their private property taken for public use without just compensation and ensure that no person can be deprived of property without due process of law?

The case was heard by Justice Irving H. Saypol. The city contested there was an unconstitutional taking and presented an expert witness to testify that the proposed skyscraper could be built at a lower cost at the site of the Biltmore.

The lawyers representing Penn Central/UGP Properties—Dewey Ballantine, Bushby, Palmer & Wood—argued that the landmark character of the building was questionable. "The esthetic quality of the south facade is obscured by its engulfment among narrow streets and high-rise buildings. It is hardly seen at all except for a short distance to the south of Park Avenue." A building on another site did not, in their analysis, provide compensatory alternatives for Penn Central and UGP Properties. During the trial they introduced evidence that Grand Central had been operating at a loss of $2 million a year for many years and therefore could not earn a reasonable return under such stringent circumstances. Penn Central also alleged that denial of the certificate to construct the Breuer plans precluded it from $1 million rent per year during the construction from UGP Properties and $3 million a year for fifty years thereafter.

The Municipal Art Society, then an eighty-year-old civic organization, made a motion to participate in the role of amicus curiae, "Friend of the Court," and produced a brief by a distinguished group of lawyers and former judges including former Mayor Robert F. Wagner; Bernard Botein, former presiding justice of the Appellate Division, State Supreme Court; Whitney North Seymour, Sr., former head of the American Bar Association; Francis T. P. Plimpton, former diplomat and former president of the Association of the Bar of the City of New York; Samuel I. Rosenman, former State Supreme Court justice and counsel to Presidents Franklin D. Roosevelt and Harry S. Truman; Bethuel M. Webster, long active in city judiciary councils; and other legal luminaries. "This is not a proposal to replace the terminal with a new facility vital to the handling of plaintiff's business or even to building a facility in addition to the terminal essential to railroad purposes. Rather it is a plan to build an office building to produce revenue." The amicus brief further argued that the plaintiff railroad received a tax exemption for the railroad portion of the terminal and that if it was in the business of owning office buildings it would need to explain how it was still entitled to a tax exemption.

As the parties anxiously awaited Justice Saypol's ruling, Roberta B. Gratz wrote in a *New York Post* article on November 8, 1974, that the city was contemplating withdrawing Grand Central's landmark designation in fear of losing the legal battle and paying Penn Central/UGP Properties damages upward of $60 million. Though Justice Saypol had not yet ruled on the matter before him, it was rumored that he was leaning toward the plaintiffs. "This was when Grand Central was really almost lost," recounted Gratz. "Kent Barwick [the executive director of the Municipal Art Society] alerted me. I wrote this story to bring to the public's attention what was going on behind the scenes. The rest is history."

When Justice Saypol handed down his opinion in January 1975, he invalidated the landmark designation of Grand Central. Though he did not question the constitutionality of the city's landmark law, he did question New York City's preventing a now-bankrupt Penn Central from earning income from the office tower addition. He determined that the landmark designation of this "long neglected faded beauty" had placed an economic hardship on the owner, who went bankrupt in 1970 but had begun the process to build in 1968 when there was a favorable office market in the Grand Central area. He also stated that the transfer of development rights of the amended zoning did not provide the railroad and the developer with commensurate compensation or minimize harm to them. The ground rent required of UGP Properties by Penn Central for a lease of the Biltmore site was $2 million more a year than the Terminal lease. Rents from an office building there would be significantly lower than at the Terminal site, which Saypol noted as a "superior location." Saypol's ruling that there was an unconstitutional taking of private property for public use without just compensation to the plaintiffs gave Penn Central the right to build either of Breuer's schemes or to demolish the Terminal in its entirety. The question of damages was severed, pending the appeal.

Many citizens of the city and historic preservationists locally and nationally reacted to the decision. "It is a tragic blow to the government's efforts to make New York a livable city," said Kent Barwick. "We think the public has a right to protect the great buildings of the past and we mean to fight for that right." "It is a soft-headed fallacy to believe that our cities exist to perpetuate a civilization," wrote Peter Blake in *New York* magazine, "or to permit us to communicate so as to create a wiser democracy. They really exist for the sole purpose of making money. . . ." It was also disclosed that the railroad's lawyers offered a deal to Mayor Abraham Beame and the City of New York. If the city didn't appeal, Penn Central would not sue for damages. If it did appeal, the railroad would demand $60 million. When news of this got out, lawyers and civic organizers knew how seductive this deal would be to a city on the verge of bankruptcy. Pressure was put on Mayor Beame to appeal the case.

Within one month of Saypol's ruling two critical events occurred that put added pressure on City Hall. Grand Central Terminal was listed in the National Register of Historic Places, which gave recognition to its significance on a national level. And, in an attempt to rally more public support and to provide New York City with additional muscle to file an appeal, the Municipal Art Society formed the Committee to Save Grand Central Station, a resolute band of citizens who promised to protect the building from the wrecking ball. With a staff of four its effectiveness grew as its lobbying became more professional and focused.

The Committee to Save Grand Central Station was composed of politicians, lawyers, celebrities, and personalities who could have paralleled the power and persuasion of the Vanderbilts in their day. Jacqueline Kennedy Onassis, Brendan Gill, Philip Johnson, Congressman Edward Koch, former Mayor Robert F. Wagner, Jimmy Breslin, Bess Meyerson, and Manhattan Borough President Percy E. Sutton were but a few of those names. Kent Barwick, Laurie Beckelman, and Frederick Papert ran the committee. (Both Barwick and Beckelman were to become chairs of the city's Landmarks Preservation Commission in later years.)

The day following Judge Saypol's 1975 decision, the *New York Times* ran a front-page story in which Municipal Art Society Executive Director Kent Barwick was named. "There we were," said Laurie Beckelman, who had joined the Municipal Art Society staff two years earlier, "just the two of us in this small office answering the phones when a soft spoken voice at the other end of the line said she'd like to speak with Kent Barwick. She said she had read the article in the *Times* and wanted to get involved. I asked her for her name and she replied, 'Jacqueline Kennedy Onassis.' I thought it was a joke. I told Kent there was a woman on the phone who claimed to be Jackie Onassis and should I take a message, to which he replied, 'no, I'll take the call.' And it really was Jackie. Kent told her that if she wanted to get involved she should join our citizens' committee. Not only did she join the committee but she called and wrote Mayor Beame to convince him to file the city's appeal. She went to the press conferences, breakfasts, whatever the event, she was there, and when she spoke it made a difference." Perhaps, as Beckelman suggested, it was Jackie's letter and phone calls to the mayor that finally convinced him to file the city's appeal.

A press conference led by Jacqueline Kennedy Onassis and Philip Johnson was held on the Oyster Bar ramp announcing the formation of the Committee to Save Grand Central Station. A national branch of the committee chaired by National Trust President James Biddle and American Institute of Architects President William Marshall, Jr., FAIA, was also announced. At the conference, architect Hugh Hardy was the leader who focused attention on the history of the Terminal and its importance architecturally, historically, and culturally. "We intend to demonstrate that Grand Central can again function as the symbol, marketplace, and economic engine with which a preeminently important part of midtown Manhattan can be rejuvenated."

Philip Johnson, in both celebrating and highlighting Jacqueline Kennedy Onassis's active participation, made the headlines when he passionately stated, "Jackie will save us." And in fact she did. The former First Lady was not participating merely as a celebrity figure. She was steeped in knowledge of the building, its architecture, and its history as well as being someone with a strong personal point of view about historic preservation. Diane Henry's piece in the *New York Times* gave an eloquent description of that day on the Oyster Bar ramp and of the woman. "I think this is so terribly important," Mrs. Onassis said, her voice barely rising over a whisper as dishes and silver rattled in the rear of the Terminal's Oyster Bar where the staff was preparing for the luncheon crowd. "We've all heard that it's too late," she said, facing the television cameras. The public has been told "that it has to happen but we know that it's not so. Even in the eleventh hour, it's not too late." Mrs. Onassis explained that she chose to help save Grand Central Terminal because "old buildings are important and if we don't care about our past, we cannot hope for our future."

Jacqueline Kennedy Onassis's commitment to preservation began long before she settled in New York. During her term as First Lady she worked in the spirit of preservation by restoring the White House. She also used her clout and became an activist for historic preservation and public architecture outside the White House gates. John Carl Warnecke, architect and friend to

the Kennedys, noted that "her focus was preserving the character that revealed
the history of our country. She had the gut instincts to know what to approve
and what not to." Historic Lafayette Square across from the White House
was saved from destruction when she stepped in to stop the bulldozers, even
though plans for new buildings had already been approved to replace the historic ones. "The wreckers haven't started yet," she said, "and until they do, it
can be saved." Without her, neither Lafayette Square nor Grand Central would
have been saved.

Though Jacqueline's involvement in the preservation of Grand Central
Terminal was positive, "it had its shortcomings," noted Gregory Gilmartin

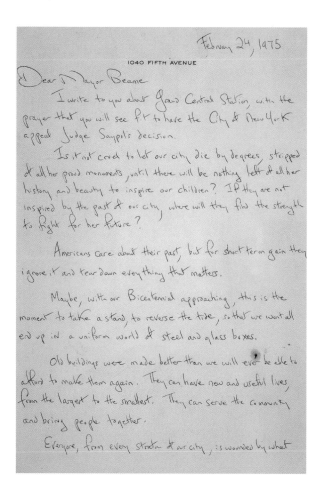

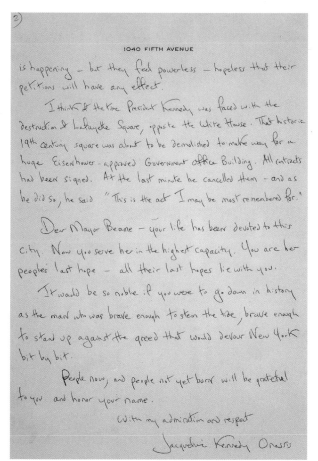

February 24, 1975

1040 FIFTH AVENUE

Dear Mayor Beame

I write to you about Grand Central Station, with the prayer that you will see fit to have the City of New York appeal Judge Saypol's decision.

Is it not cruel to let our city die by degrees, stripped of all her proud monuments, until there will be nothing left of all her history and beauty to inspire our children? If they are not inspired by the past of our city, where will they find the strength to fight for her future?

Americans care about their past, but for short term gain they ignore it and tear down everything that matters.

Maybe, with our Bicentennial approaching, this is the moment to take a stand, to reverse the tide, so that we won't all end up in a uniform world of steel and glass boxes.

Old buildings were made better than we will ever be able to afford to make them again. They can have new and useful lives, from the largest to the smallest. They can serve the community and bring people together.

Everyone, from every strata of our city, is wounded by what

1040 FIFTH AVENUE

is happening — but they feel powerless — hopeless that their petitions will have any effect.

I think of the time President Kennedy was faced with the destruction of Lafayette Square, opposite the White House. That historic 19th century square was about to be demolished to make way for a huge Eisenhower-approved Government office Building. All contracts had been signed. At the last minute he cancelled them — and as he did so, he said "This is the act I may be most remembered for."

Dear Mayor Beame — your life has been devoted to this city. Now you serve her in the highest capacity. You are her people's last hope — all their last hopes lie with you.

It would be so noble if you were to go down in history as the man who was brave enough to stem the tide, brave enough to stand up against the greed that would devour New York bit by bit.

People now, and people not yet born will be grateful to you and honor your name.

With my admiration and respect

Jacqueline Kennedy Onassis

Jacqueline Kennedy Onassis's handwritten letter to Mayor Abraham Beame was an impassioned plea to save Grand Central.
© Caroline Kennedy Schlossberg/John F. Kennedy Library

in his book about the Municipal Art Society, *Shaping the City*. "Some used Mrs. Onassis' involvement to paint preservation as the hobby of people who never rode the subways. But these were far outweighed by the advantages. Jacqueline Onassis brought to the Municipal Art Society a visceral belief in preservation . . . she attracted news cameras as a flame draws moths. People hesitated to rebuff her. They took her phone calls."

The Committee to Save Grand Central had a clear strategy: to create a vehement public outcry and turn the tide of opposition. It was the time of the bicentennial and Grand Central was becoming a symbol people could relate to. The building's plight was known as far away as India, Greece, and Turkey. The committee set up a storefront office in the Biltmore Hotel at 43rd and Vanderbilt across the street from Grand Central Terminal and created fliers and newsletters to paper the streets and flood the offices of politicians. Citizens of New York were entreated to either join the committee, volunteer their time, send money, or start petition drives. "Only a strong public protest can keep Grand Central from going under," one of the pamphlets read. "This case is a test of our civic pride—our sense of history and our appreciation of the amenities we have in the present. Little by little, many of our finest landmarks are becoming endangered species. New York has much to be proud of and Grand Central Station is one of its proudest monuments. Let's save it!"

Free tours were conducted every week (the free tours still take place every Wednesday at 12:30 P.M.) to audiences that sometimes included up to forty people on their lunch hour. One of the volunteer tour guides, Barry Lewis, would begin in his thick New York accent with something reminiscent of "This is the famous view of NYC since 1913 and we want to save it," followed by improvisational interplay with people sharing personal memories of the station that ranged from tearful good-byes to merely standing on the balcony, watching the crowds.

As the committee's actions heated up, more debates and commentaries were taking place in the press. Newspaper editorials accused members of the Municipal Art Society and the Committee to Save Grand Central of trying to save a spirit that was long gone and merely a fantasy of their own creation. A newspaper editorial stated that saving Grand Central was as absurd and impossible as having a Walden Pond in New York. The real estate community predicted that preservationists would take control of the city and, by landmarking everything they could, would push developers out of New York and into the suburbs and turn a decaying city center into a ghetto. Doris Freedman, an important board member of the Municipal Art Society, led a counterattack to this negative publicity by contacting Congressman Ed Koch for support on the federal level. Freedman was one of Koch's earliest supporters in his mayoral campaign and persuaded him to work behind the scenes rallying support from the Metropolitan Transportation Authority (MTA), which had leased Grand Central Terminal in 1972.

While the drama was being played out in both the legal and the public arena, New York City's economy was nearing bankruptcy and Penn Central was going to rack and ruin financially. There were people who argued that, in this business climate, a new skyscraper atop Grand Central Terminal was not economically feasible; therefore, Grand Central was not realistically in any imminent

Mayor Abraham Beame, Beverly Moss Spatt, Jacqueline Kennedy Onassis, and Percy Sutton join forces in the landmarks battle.

AP/Wide World Photos

threat. But preservationists, civic leaders, and passionate citizens believed there was a need to protect the building before the city's economics gained momentum again as well as permanently secure the landmark law.

When Mayor Beame agreed to have the city file an appeal to Judge Saypol's ruling, he also agreed to have the city's best legal talent on the case. His Corporation Counsel chose Nina Gershon Goldstein, one of the attorneys within the appeals division of the city law department who cared deeply about environmental concerns. "The really important thing was Nina's attitude. She felt the city should and could win and brought incredible determination, energy, and strength to the case," Dorothy Miner recounted. Trained as both a lawyer and a planner, Miner brought her own unique insight to the case, first as a volunteer and subsequently as counsel at the Landmarks Commission. One of the main issues Miner impressed upon her colleagues was the need to look at landmarking not as something selectively focused on a single property but as another form of land-use regulation. Like building, zoning, and health codes, landmarking should be addressed as another code that was part of the city's overall land-use policy. "I'm not trying to take away from Jackie or the amicus brief by MAS," Miner stated firmly, "but the main work and briefs were done by the city's law department. It was Nina Gershon Goldstein who came up with the argument about the failure to include imputed value for the space used for the railroad. She came up with a series of arguments that disputed Saypol's findings that there wasn't a reasonable return. This was truly one of the great cases of the city's law department."

Beverly Moss Spatt was the chairperson of the Landmarks Preservation Commission at the time of the appeal. Behind her and the city's Law Department was a dedicated group of public-spirited lawyers working behind the scenes to prepare the amicus briefs supporting the landmarks law and the preservation of Grand Central. Ralph Menapace, general counsel for the Municipal Art Society, assembled a legal team consisting of, among others, Jack Kerr, Paul Byard, and Peter Sloan to write the Society's and the American Institute of Architects' amicus brief in the appeals process. There were also other briefs filed by the New York State attorney general and the Citizens Housing and Planning Council of New York. These efforts complemented the more visible support given to the city by civic organizations and public figures.

The Grand Central case was a defining moment in the historic preservation movement from a legal perspective. It is the case that set the standard for all preservation cases to come, and the work of Ralph Menapace, Whitney North Seymour, Sr., and Dorothy Miner marked the coming of age of a new generation of lawyers who would devote themselves pro bono publico to keeping the architecture of our heritage.

Menapace, Seymour, and their teams met often with the amicus groups and the city's Law Department to strategize and frame the legal arguments. This pool of talented lawyers with different legal specialties lent their experience and skills to aid the city in research and ideas. Ralph Menapace, whose corporate legal experience was different than most of the city's lawyers in the Law Department, had the personality and the ability to bring new perspectives to the effort. Whitney North Seymour, Sr., at that time was one of the great lions of the bar and the former head of the American Bar Association. He had argued many important cases in the Supreme Court and appellate courts across the country, and he held many honors and distinctions. He lent his prestigious name and his experience with the courts to the Grand Central case just as it moved into the crucial appellate stage. The men were very different. Seymour was the great public speaker, and Menapace was the modest but effective strategist behind the scenes. The supporting army of young lawyers and protégés who sat at the feet of these two masters would continue the preservation battle beyond Grand Central—including Jack Kerr, who, after working with Menapace and then Seymour, later joined the New York Landmarks Conservancy Board and carried the tradition to subsequent preservation cases like that of St. Bartholomew's Church.

Justice Saypol had severed the question of damages while the city appealed his decision on the constitutionality of the city's actions. Some two dozen Grand Central supporters, organized by the Municipal Art Society, attended the appeals hearing in October 1975 as a silent but forceful presence in a small courtroom in lower Manhattan. On December 16, 1975, the city won a three-to-two decision in the Appellate Division of the Supreme Court of the State of New York, reversing Saypol's decision, upholding the constitutionality of the Landmarks Preservation Commission's denial of the permit application, and dismissing the complaint. The court found that the plaintiffs had failed to establish that the landmarks regulation had deprived them of all reasonable beneficial use of their property; Penn Central was denied the right to build atop Grand Central.

Writing for the majority Justice Francis T. Murphy stated, in an eleven-page opinion, "The need to preserve structures worthy of landmark status is beyond dispute." Justice Murphy, addressing the issue of Penn Central/UGP Properties claims of economic hardship, went on to say that "it is their burden to establish that they are incapable of obtaining a reasonable return from Grand Central Terminal operations, not that they are not receiving it . . . in our view such burden has not been met."

The dissent to the majority opinion written by Justice Lupiano stated that without the office tower above Grand Central, the building "is incapable of producing a reasonable economic return."

The victory for preservation and the city was met with ebullience. The December ruling, touted as a Christmas present to the city of New York, was barely unwrapped when the railroad decided to appeal *this* reversal to the state's highest court, the New York Court of Appeals in Albany.

In January 1976 Margot Wellington succeeded Kent Barwick as executive director of the Municipal Art Society. Shortly afterward she was approached by the advertising agency J. Walter Thompson offering to help with pro bono services. The agency came up with the slogan "No More Bites Out of the Big

Apple." Buttons and Grand Central T-shirts were sold, free apples were passed out on the street, and ties were designed with little apples, each with a bite missing.

When the New York Court of Appeals case was being prepared, Nina Gershon Goldstein was no longer in the Appeals division of the city's Law Department. Her colleague, Leonard Koerner, took over and argued the case, working closely with Dorothy Miner, who had been hired by the city to become the Landmarks Commission's full-time counsel. Mayor Abraham Beame and Jacqueline Kennedy Onassis with the Committee to Save Grand Central Station, alongside performers Jerry Ohrbach, Tammy Grimes, Kay Medford, and Bobby Short, rallied in front of the statue of Commodore Vanderbilt (on the south side of the terminal) on April 21, 1977, one week before the New York Court of Appeals heard oral arguments.

On June 23, 1977, the Court of Appeals unanimously upheld the order of the Appellate Division. The court wrote in support of its decision that the "economic return of Grand Central should include an imputed value based on the increased business in the hotels and office buildings owned by Penn Central which is generated by the presence of the Terminal" and that the development rights could be transferred to a number of other properties owned by Penn Central.

Penn Central/UGP Properties had exhausted the New York appeals process. Their final option was to have the case heard by the United States Supreme Court. Grand Central was the first land-use regulation case of any type to reach the Supreme Court in two decades and the first that considered the merits of a landmarks preservation law.

The "Landmark Express" full of preservationists bound for Washington, D.C., to support Grand Central's case.

Courtesy of the Municipal Art Society of New York

Prior to the case being accepted by the Supreme Court, Penn Central/UGP Properties filed in September 1977 what is known as a jurisdictional statement in which they argued why the Court should take this case. They reiterated the claim that to preserve social and cultural desirability of landmarks through government regulations constituted the "taking" of private property for public use without just compensation in violation of the Constitution. In response, New York City argued that there was no need for the Supreme Court to take the case as it was really a matter of municipal law that had been upheld unanimously by the highest court in New York. It reiterated that the overall scheme of landmarking in New York City distinguishes landmark designation from discriminatory or "spot" zoning. The Supreme Court agreed to take the case, at which point the city and Penn

Central/UGP Properties prepared their briefs with support from amicus briefs.

The Pacific Legal Foundation and the New York Real Estate Board filed amicus briefs in support of Penn Central's position. The Solicitor General of the United States, the states of New York and California, the Committee to Save Grand Central Station, the National Trust for Historic Preservation, the Municipal Art Society, the New York Landmarks Conservancy, the cities of New Orleans, Boston, and San Antonio, and a number of other conservation and preservation groups filed briefs in support of New York City's position. The battle to save Grand Central was not just about one building. If this battle was lost, it would present a real threat to preservation laws throughout America.

The new round of briefing by the opposing sides was joined by rigorous campaigning. The Municipal Art Society and the Committee to Save Grand Central came up with a highly creative and unusual ploy to gain public support and judicial attention. On April 17 they orchestrated a train trip to Washington that rivaled the best trips of politicians on the campaign trail. Billed as the "whistle-stop crusade" on the "Landmark Express," this one-day Amtrak excursion began in New York's new Penn Station and picked up preservation-supportive passengers in Philadelphia; Wilmington, Delaware; and Baltimore. Led by Jacqueline Kennedy Onassis; Frederick Papert; Brendan Gill, then the theater critic of *The New Yorker*, Philip Johnson; and Henry Geldzahler, the city's cultural affairs commissioner, a group of over 300 devotees of Grand Central filled an eight-car entourage.

A press conference by Mayor Ed Koch held at Grand Central was the kickoff to this four-hour adventure to Washington. Passengers were fed donated hamburgers and fries courtesy of McDonald's, and were entertained by a classical trio, two mimes, a pair of clowns from the Big Apple Circus School, fire-eating jugglers, and a strolling banjo player. Adding to this carnival atmosphere were volunteers running though the trains handing out blue and white "Save Grand Central" balloons, T-shirts, and buttons. Over the loudspeaker passengers sang their personal hymn to the building to the tune of "Tipperary."

Let's make a grand stand to save Grand Central, the greatest landmark site of all.
It's a great part of New York City like the lights of old Broadway
Let's make a grand, grand stand for Grand Central, for the good old U.S.A.

SUNDAY, APRIL 16th

Make tracks to D.C. to save Grand Central!

GRAND CENTRAL is imperiled again. A landmark decision is in the hands of the U.S. Supreme Court. We must demonstrate our concern. Join Jackie Onassis, Brendan Gill and other celebrities for a non-stop celebration to preserve Grand Central Station

A Municipal Art Society poster announces the train trip from New York to Washington to show support for the Terminal's case that was before the Supreme Court.

Courtesy of the Municipal Art Society of New York

A Main Concourse crowd watches intently as a performance sponsored by the Committee to Save Grand Central Station raises public awareness of its cause.

© Neal Boenzi/NYT Pictures

This enthusiastic crowd was met in Washington by Senator Daniel Patrick Moynihan and Joan Mondale, wife of the vice president. When Jacqueline Kennedy Onassis was asked why she was so actively involved in this she answered, "If Grand Central Station goes, all of the landmarks in this country will go as well. If that happens, we'll live in a world of steel and glass. This is an issue that represents all issues. If this one goes, they all go. . . ."

Frederick Papert, who with Margot Wellington and Laurie Beckelman was one of the event orchestrators for the Municipal Art Society, believed the Supreme Court would uphold Grand Central's landmark status. In recalling the famous train trip to Washington, D.C., Papert's most vivid memory was of their arrival in the nation's capital. With the First Lady's return to Washington, it was as if Camelot had come home. "People came out on that day to see Jackie," Papert recounted. "Mrs. Mondale, Senator Moynihan were two powerful Washington presences, but they loomed in the background once she appeared. But it didn't matter because in coming to see her, people came in droves, they saw, they heard, we won! 'Jackie would save us,' Philip Johnson said at the beginning of our crusade. Perhaps on that day she did."

Not everyone was enthusiastic about the whistle-stop train crusade. Many at the city Law Department and others in the legal profession were offended at the idea of turning a moment of judicial history into a crudely orchestrated event designed apparently to influence the justices of the Supreme Court by swaying public opinion. Even Whitney North Seymour, Sr., who had organized the Municipal Art Society's team of lawyers, was purportedly concerned when he discovered that the train trip was to occur.

Though the lawyer for Penn Central/UGP Properties, Daniel M. Gribbon, Esq., of the firm Covington & Burling, reargued many of the same points previously brought before the three courts in New York, he now put even greater emphasis on the violation of his client's Fifth Amendment rights. One of the primary purposes of the Fifth Amendment is to ensure fairness in the impact of government upon owners of private property. The denial of the use of the air rights for the office tower was a taking of those air rights, thus a taking of part of Penn Central's property by the city. Property could not be "taken" without just compensation. This was an exceedingly complex constitutional concept that had been violated, stated Gribbon to the justices. Gribbon went on to say that it was his view that neither the Court of Appeals nor New York City had taken into consideration the fairness concept, which in turn resulted in the burden of the cost of preservation being passed to Penn Central instead of to the public as a whole.

Joan Mondale speaks at the rally at Union Station in Washington, D.C. Standing behind her from left to right are Fred Papert, Jacqueline Kennedy Onassis, and Brendan Gill.

Courtesy of the Municipal Art Society of New York

In his oral argument on behalf of the city, Leonard Koerner argued that property had not been "taken" without fair compensation. "The nub of the case," stated Koerner, "was that Grand Central has not been singled out. There was a landmark law in place before the announcement that Penn Central was going to build on top of Grand Central." He went on to say, "This case must therefore be judged on the basis that Grand Central is indeed profitable in its present use as a railroad for passenger service and that part of the issue regarding air rights was whether the $3.8 million return on the Biltmore site was so unfair as to emasculate the land use regulation, not whether Penn Central was entitled to the highest and best use."

Dorothy Miner, present at the hearing, noted how Koerner captured the borderline justices. "During Lenny Koerner's oral argument they had a great number of questions. What he's good at is answering the question while bringing them back to what he wanted to argue as he moved it forward. That's a very adept lawyer and one of the most important characteristics of appearing before the Supreme Court. It's one of the times when oral arguments really mattered. His answers, not the whistle stop train, made the decision what it was. He showed the justices that if the railroad ever closed down and stopped using the Terminal we would have another set of facts and they would be entitled to come back. And that was the most critical thing of all in terms of proving fairness."

The oral arguments were concluded by Patricia M. Wald, speaking on behalf of the United States as amicus curiae, on the government's commitment to historic preservation and the national policy. She declared that "historical and cultural foundations of the nation should be preserved as a living part of our community life and development in order to give our people a sense of orientation."

At the conclusion of the oral arguments the case was submitted to the Supreme Court on April 17, 1978. On June 26 the Supreme Court settled in a thirty-one-page opinion any question that laws passed to save historic buildings advanced a legitimate public interest and thus were a legal use. It also upheld the landmark status of Grand Central and the commission's denial of the permit to construct an office tower atop the Terminal.

Justice William J. Brennan delivered the opinion of the Court in the 6–3 decision. "Over the past 50 years, all 50 states and over 500 municipalities have enacted laws to encourage or require the preservation of buildings and areas with historic or aesthetic importance. These nationwide legislative efforts have been precipitated by two concerns. The first is recognition that, in recent years, large numbers of historic structures, landmarks, and areas have been destroyed without adequate consideration of either the values represented therein or the possibility of preserving the destroyed properties for use in economically productive ways. The second is a widely shared belief that structures with special historic, cultural, or architectural significance enhance the quality of life for all. Not only do these buildings and their workmanship represent the lessons of the past and embody precious features of our heritage, they serve as examples of quality for today." Brennan notes in the opinion that "it is, of course, true that the fact the duties imposed by zoning and historic-district legislation apply throughout particular physical communities provides assurances against arbitrariness, but the applicability of the Landmarks Law to a large number of parcels in the city, in our view, provides comparable, if not identical, assurances." The Supreme Court accepted Koerner's argument on behalf of the city of New York that local landmark regulation served a substantial public purpose and was a legitimate basis for regulating land use. Rejecting the claim that the air rights were a separate property and had been totally taken, Brennan stated that the application of the landmarks law did not interfere with the historic use of the landmark as a terminal and that the record recognized that Penn Central was permitted a reasonable beneficial use of the landmark. The landmarks law had not effected a taking. The Court concluded that Penn Central/UGP Properties' Fifth Amendment rights had therefore not been violated.

Associate Justice William H. Rehnquist wrote for the minority in dissent, "If the cost of preserving Grand Central Terminal were spread evenly across the entire population of the City of New York, the burden per person would be in cents per year, a minor cost that the city would surely concede for the benefit accrued." But instead, Justice Rehnquist said, the city "would impose the entire cost of several million dollars per year on Penn Central—but it is precisely this sort of discrimination that the Fifth Amendment prohibits." Joining in the Rehnquist dissent were Chief Justice Warren E. Burger and Associate Justice John Paul Stevens. The dissent states that "property is taken in the constitutional sense when inroads are made upon an owner's use of it to an extent that, as between private parties, a servitude has been acquired. Unlike other zoning issues where the burden is shared . . . here a multimillion loss has been imposed on appellants and not offset by any benefits flowing from the preservation of some 400 other landmarks in NYC."

The decision was met with jubilance by the city, its citizens, and preservationists across the country.

The ink was barely dry on the ruling when preservationists began making plans to use the Grand Central ruling by the nation's highest court to save other landmarks. After the Supreme Court decision came down the real estate community said that it might be constitutional but it didn't seem fair. The *Wall Street Journal* ominously predicted that "landmark designation is enough to discourage the purchase of historical structures, and current owners have strong incentives to demolish them. "Penn Central/UGP Properties petitioned the Supreme Court for a rehearing but did not succeed. And the Municipal Art Society, once a small but visible group, had become a popular civic force with, like the city's own legal group, a newfound respect.

Nearly two decades after the final Supreme Court ruling, Grand Central Terminal was being restored to its original grandeur without a weighty neighbor atop its shoulders, and when one of Grand Central's greatest supporters died, she was honored within the very walls she had saved from demolition. On a weekend morning in 1994, as the sun shone through the windows in the newly restored waiting room, with its warm, muted, caen stone walls and newly restored chandeliers, there stood two books, two lines, and dozens of people of all ages and economic and ethnic backgrounds waiting to sign the memorial book for Jackie.

When Grand Central Terminal was rededicated on October 1, 1998, it was not hard to understand why so many had fought so hard to save the Terminal. On that day, 5,000 people filled the Main Concourse, which had been returned to its original grandeur. Many were thanked, many remembered, but even twenty years after the Supreme Court decision it was the name of Jacqueline Kennedy Onassis that shone as brightly as the constellations on the newly restored celestial ceiling.

CHAPTER TWO

LIFE BEFORE THE TERMINAL

. . . young men were in full motion toward their changes, their tasks, their fortunes: a whole continent to plunder, "teeming with treasure," a vast network of railways to be built.
—MATTHEW JOSEPHSON, *THE ROBBER BARONS*

The 1913 Grand Central Terminal, with its classical arches and cathedral-like interior, had a lineage of other buildings on this site that rivaled its grandness: the 1871 Grand Central Depot and the 1898 Station. The Depot was one of the finest examples of post–Civil War architecture. Its presence created an unprecedented change in New York City that was part of a renaissance in America's commercial and industrial history.

The commercial inimitability of 1830s New York was based on its access to an unsurpassed system of water transportation, with its natural harbor's coastal and transatlantic shipping. As a result, growing steamboat services operating on the Hudson River linked the city and its harbor with upstate New York and the Great Lakes via the Erie Canal. Water transport was effective but limited as the growth of the country expanded well beyond the natural limits of geographical access by water. This led to another form of travel, the iron roads, whose tracks could be extended effortlessly, unlike the canals, which had to be dredged. The commercial rails that were growing throughout Britain and Europe became a model for an infrastructure of railroads that spread swiftly across the United States.

With the growing interest in rail transport across the country, New York City too would have its new railroads and its new industrialists. This convergence was exemplified by the millionaire steamboat tycoon Cornelius Vanderbilt, whose vision led not only to rail expansion throughout the country but also to the creation of the Grand Central Depot. But the full impact of rail as the prime source of travel would not be realized until after the Civil War. The end of the Civil War set the stage for the creation of a new country. The war abolished slavery, cemented the Union of the States, and ushered in an unprecedented age

Looking east along 42nd Street, an 1886 photograph shows the midday activity outside the Depot.
Courtesy of MTA/Metro-North Collection

In forming the mighty New York Central and Hudson River Railroad Company, Vanderbilt singlehandedly merged many lines into one continuous railroad.

Courtesy of MTA/Metro-North Collection

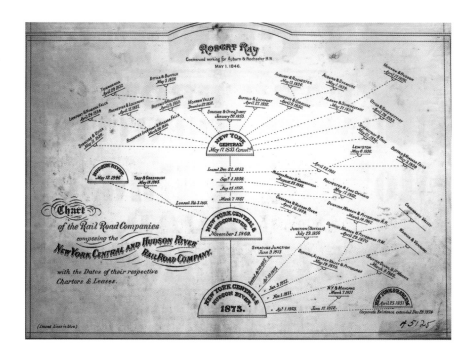

A railroad crew poses with their steam locomotive, circa 1860.

Collection of New York Central System Historical Society Inc.

of ambitious visions of growth, wealth, power, and industrialization. The brutality and determination of the battlefield continued on in a new breed of soldiers —soldiers of capital or, as they would come to be known, captains of industry.

The domination of wealth based on the value of a crop or herd, or the amount of land one owned and cultivated, was over. Men like Cornelius Vanderbilt, Jim Fisk, John D. Rockefeller, Daniel Drew, and Andrew Carnegie took center stage and became known as the robber barons. Laissez-faire government policies created dynasties of great personal fortunes and monopolies. There were no antitrust laws to offer hope to small or new businesses, no income taxes that would require payment proportionate to one's wealth, and no laws to regulate hours or wages. Industrialization became the propellant of social development and international prominence; the dark side of this growth, sweatshops and unlivable wages, was never challenged. "The eight years in America from 1860 to 1868," wrote Mark Twain in *The Gilded Age*, "uprooted institutions that were centuries old, changed the politics of a people, transformed the social life of half the country, and wrought so profoundly upon the entire national character that the influence cannot be measured short of two or three generations."

From 1850 to the end of the century, American railroads grew from 9,000 miles to 193,000 miles of tracks. Cities were built, communities formed, and the population multiplied as people rode the rails. As each section of the track was laid, the nation increased in size and power. In New York, railroad companies such as the Attica and Buffalo, the Syracuse and Attica, and the Utica and Syracuse connected the cities of their names. In 1853 they merged into the New York Central Railroad, harnessing ten lines into one that ran between Albany and Buffalo. It was the first major consolidation of lines and signaled the economy-ruling railroad companies that were to come. Vanderbilt, a bold, coarse, crafty figure, would lead the pack of high-powered industrialists.

Though Vanderbilt's commitment to the seas gained him the name "Commodore," the man who had dominated the steamboat business on the Hudson River foresaw an empire of a great continuous railroad line extending from New York to the West, something none of his contemporaries had dared to dream. In 1863, while his competitors were looking in other directions, he began acquiring control of the New York and Harlem Railroad, which ran from Chatham Four Corners to 42nd Street. Vanderbilt convinced the city government, then the corrupt organization of "Boss Tweed" Tammany Hall, to approve the extension of the line from 42nd Street to the Battery. He also had the support of the federal government because of all the Union soldiers he'd transported by sea during the Civil War. This extra line on 42nd Street increased the value of the Harlem Railroad exponentially and marked the first major accomplishment of the Commodore as a railroad man. One year later he purchased a controlling interest in the Hudson River Railroad. Through stock acquisitions, the Hudson Line was commandeered by Vanderbilt, who then sought to merge his two lines.

Vanderbilt acquired a large block of stock in the New York Central, which at that time extended across the state of New York from Albany to Buffalo.

A lithograph of "Commodore" Cornelius Vanderbilt, founder of the New York Central Railroad.
Courtesy of MTA/Metro-North Collection

Daniel Drew, a railroad investor and rival, tried to block any additional acquisitions by Vanderbilt, but failed. One year after his showdown with Drew and the New York Central, Vanderbilt had gained full control of the railroad. Using his Hudson Line as leverage, on January 15 Vanderbilt denied any New York Central cargo to use the tracks to New York City during the uncommonly cold winter of 1867–68. Because of the ice, the New York Central could not reach the city by water or by railroad, causing the stock value of the line to plummet. Vanderbilt bought up more of the stock, gained a seat on the board of directors, and eventually became the line's president.

In New York, Vanderbilt began to lay the groundwork to control the routes into New York, the ultimate destination for both passengers and freight. Freight traveled down the west side of Manhattan to St. John's Park Depot, a three-story utilitarian stone building constructed for the Hudson River Railroad in 1868. It was adorned by a massive bronze statue of the Commodore outfitted in his characteristic astrakhan fur coat and sporting his distinctively bushy sideburns. The statue now lives on in front of Grand Central Terminal, gazing down Park Avenue South. Passenger trains merged at Fourth Avenue on the east side of town and continued south to 42nd Street, where they terminated at the existing Harlem Railroad Depot between 42nd and 45th streets. Vanderbilt acquired this fully operating depot, consisting of a car house, locomotive house, stable, cattle shed, blacksmith, and small passenger area, in the Harlem Railroad takeover. More importantly it gave him ownership of the parcel of land that was to become the busiest acreage in the world and the most valuable of his assets. His was now the only railroad with a direct route into Manhattan, making his operation more time and cost effective.

With growing congestion in lower Manhattan, the number of accidents between New York Central and Hudson River Railroad trains, trolley cars, and pedestrians rapidly accelerated.

Railroad Magazine. Courtesy of William D. Middleton

In 1856 New York banned train travel south of 42nd Street because of an inordinate number of accidents between trains and pedestrians. Subsequently, passengers got out of the Depot and continued by horse-drawn trolley for a forty-five-minute ride downtown. Although accidents declined, railroad demand did not. With the increase in ridership and the demands of commerce, the terminus of the Hudson River and Harlem Lines had become inadequate.

The facility was not designed for such abundant activity, and arrival and departure delays soon became commonplace. By the end of the decade, Vanderbilt's amalgamation of railroad companies boasted a fleet of 408 locomotives, 445 passenger cars, 132 baggage cars, and 9,026 freight cars that all rolled across 740 miles of track. This growing fleet was in need of a central depot to unite

the lines and to gather and welcome all passengers. It would need to be a formidable structure, to represent the prowess of the three railroads: the New York Central, the Hudson, and the Harlem.

The site selected for Vanderbilt's new Grand Central Depot was the Harlem's existing steam locomotive facilities between East 42nd and 45th streets. Bordering the west side of this new depot, Fifth Avenue was becoming transformed into a fashionable thoroughfare that would ultimately have elaborate dwellings for the Astors, Stewarts, and Vanderbilts. The east side, once rolling farmland, was rapidly being transformed into slums such as the infamous Dutch Hill, an area of breweries, slaughterhouses, warehouses, and immigrant housing, representing the other end of the city's social gamut. The site for Vanderbilt's new railroad depot marked the social boundary between these two extremes.

Its location was quickly criticized by the public as being "at the end of the earth," since most of Manhattan's population and urban center was downtown. Forty-second Street was one of New York's "uptown" thoroughfares, widened from river to river for the services that connected the ferries. Vanderbilt's foresight of tomorrow's New York spanning the entire island made the proposed site a very sensible choice. By this time, New York's population was approaching one million and Vanderbilt knew the growth would have to be northward. That, combined with a lack of appropriate real estate farther south and the city's prohibition against steam locomotives south of 42nd Street, caused Vanderbilt to rule out a lower Manhattan site. With his persuasive conviction, Vanderbilt received the city's approval to close Fourth Avenue at 42nd Street, a decision that truly made the depot the center of attention.

The year 1869 was monumental for the Commodore. He completed mergers of the New York Central Railroad, the Hudson River Railroad, and the Harlem Railroad, and extended their territory of operations as far west as Chicago through one amalgamation after another. This resulted in the most powerful transportation company of its day. And in the summer of that year, excavation began for the Grand Central Depot.

Vanderbilt had a vision of a railroad depot that would greatly enhance public transportation as well as urban development. This vision was supported by the city's own interests. The approving legislation of 1869 stated that Grand Central Depot would "be constructed of the best materials, and the front of said buildings on 42nd Street shall be of Philadelphia pressed brick, brown or free-stone, or marble and iron, and shall be furnished in the best style of architecture." The city's leaders were well aware of the potential civic and cultural value of Vanderbilt's building.

Construction began in the fall of 1869 and provided an income to the residents of the immigrant housing to the east of the depot. For two years they excavated the site, stacked the bricks, and raised the iron trusses. On October 9, 1871, Grand Central Depot was completed, and it dominated the area of 42nd Street.

The architect of the Depot, John B. Snook, was a respected designer known for A. T. Stewart's department store at 280 Broadway in lower Manhattan and the St. John's Freight Depot for the Hudson River Railroad. Grand Central Depot was a formidable presence in a rapidly growing area of the City. It had a trio of towers, representing the three lines that used the depot: the New

An 1876 watercolor illustrates the early development of 42nd Street when it was considered to be "at the end of the earth." Grand Central Depot, a Victorian style church, a Romanesque style health institute, and Mrs. White's rolling goat farm (which decades later became the location of the Chrysler Building) are all along the north side of 42nd Street.

Courtesy of the Museum of the City of New York

As shown in this view looking east along
42nd Street, the dignified presence of
Vanderbilt's Grand Central Depot in the
French Empire style dominates the rapid
development of midtown Manhattan.
(circa 1870s)

ERECTED 1871

ARCHITECTURAL IRON WORKS

3225

The north-facing façade of the train shed, built for the steam-driven locomotives that still used Grand Central Station.

Corbis/Hulton-Deutsch ©

York and Hudson, the New York and Harlem, and the New York and New Haven. The red brick masonry, classical fenestration, and ornamental ironwork (painted white to appear as marble) made a statement of strength and dignity but were actually chosen for their fireproof qualities and durability. Although these types of elaborate facades and massive sheds were rising throughout Paris, London, Milan, and Berlin, they were virtually unknown in America at the time. So when Grand Central Depot was complete, it was, in the words of architectural historian Carroll L. V. Meeks, "one of the first American stations capable of standing comparison with the finest European ones."

The L-shaped structure surrounding the train shed, which emulated Paddington Station in London, was called the head house and at street level contained all the services that passengers required: waiting rooms, ticket offices, restaurants, newsstands, and restrooms on the 42nd Street side and alternate waiting rooms and baggage facilities on the Vanderbilt Avenue side. On the upper two floors were the railroad company offices. The Depot was intentionally designed to face the more affluent parts of the city to the south and west, having its most attractive facades along 42nd Street and Vanderbilt Avenue.

As glorious as the head house was, in both its external and its internal features, the wonder of the building was to be found in the great train shed, said to have been copied from the St. Pancras Station in London. Inspired by the great arched roofs of the midcentury European railway stations, train sheds were spectacular feats of engineering design that became symbols of the new technology of travel. Snook, with his engineers Issac Buckhout and R. G. Hatfield, designed a train shed that was to become one of the country's most popular tourist destinations, second only to the U.S. Capitol. Thirty-two wrought-iron trusses, each spanning 200 feet and rising up almost 100 feet, formed a semicircular arch that covered an area of 652 feet from head house to train yard. Covered with thousands of panes of glass, the roof created a Crystal Palace effect. With the interior illuminated at night by gas lamps, a majestic glow radiated throughout the lofty space. Grand Central Depot was received with enthusiasm by the press and the public. "The largest railway and passenger caravansary in the world," touted the *New York Herald* on June 30, 1871.

Beneath this vault of iron and glass lay 12 tracks and 7 platforms, handling 85 trains each day during the Depot's first year of operation. Yet despite the great technological advances that produced such exciting architecture, the train sheds were difficult places to keep clean. Smoke and cinders gushed from the engine stacks of the locomotives, filling the sheds' interior and blackening all surfaces. Vanderbilt and his railroad staff were proud of their architectural creation and industrial achievement, and they were not going to allow their monument to be dirtied. As Carl Condit claimed, "Cornelius Vanderbilt and his immediate successors possessed a laudable devotion to cleanliness, which revealed itself in their aim to keep the station free of smoke." Vanderbilt and his engineers developed a system called "flying in" to keep the smoke out of the train shed. As a train approached the depot, the engine would separate and accelerate away from the cars. Next the engine would be directed to a side track

William Sonntag's watercolor *Between the Tracks* (circa 1880) depicts the mystique of train travel as the cars line up on a rainy night in the track yard behind the north facade of the Depot.

Courtesy of The Adirondack Museum

and the remainder of the train would glide into the train shed. A brakeman could then bring the train to a smooth, smoke-free halt. Departures were far less of a problem, since the locomotive was repositioned close to the outside end of the enclosed train shed. The railroad company was also conscious of excessive noise in this vast space. Bells on departing trains were banned and whistles were used only in emergencies.

As the New York Central and Hudson River Railroad company was thriving in the new Grand Central Depot, times were not as good in other parts of the country. The 1871 fire that devastated Chicago affected the financial world and caused a major crash in the New York Stock Exchange. Dominated by railroad stock, the Stock Exchange experienced the waves of fear rippling through the railroad industry. The Commodore, now almost eighty, was still at the helm of the New York Central, and his son, William H. Vanderbilt, was being brought up through the ranks of the company. William did not possess the brute force and the fearful commanding presence of his father, but he was quite adept at general management and business expansion. Amid labor uproars in neighboring regions, William Vanderbilt retained his workforce by cutting the salaries of all employees, including high-paid executives, and offering in return $100,000 to be divided among the most loyal employees when the economy regained its health.

Ticket agents and porters pose in Grand Central Station's waiting room with the train shed's glass roof behind them, circa 1900.
Courtesy of MTA/Metro-North Collection

Climbing to a height of almost 100 feet above the tracks, the ornate iron trusses of the Depot's shed dwarfed the trains below. Over 600 feet long and one of the largest interior spaces in North America in the nineteenth century, Grand Central Depot was a much visited tourist attraction, second only to the U.S. Capitol in popularity.
Courtesy of MTA/Metro-North Collection

The father and son team began to build on their mighty empire during this time of waning prosperity. They expanded the rails to Ohio, Indiana, and Illinois, working toward a continuous route between New York and Chicago. They acquired vulnerable stocks, which helped them move toward that goal. They also joined forces with the U.S. government to establish an express mail service between New York and Chicago. William H. Vanderbilt arranged the deal, and a spectacular train was designed that could deliver mail in one working day. The service, though a giant leap in communications and business affairs, lasted only ten months. It was later reestablished with a similar train in 1877 that existed for many years.

Grand Central Depot handled more and more travelers, as lines expanded to connect New York City to formerly distant regions. The early years of the Depot's existence proved effective and worthy, for it was, as architectural historian Carl Condit acclaimed, "the first American terminal fully planned in its functional, aesthetic, and symbolic character for the needs of the rising nineteenth century metropolis."

William H. Vanderbilt, the oldest son of the "Commodore," continued the Vanderbilt railroad legacy.

Corbis/Oscar White ©

This cartoon of William H. Vanderbilt depicts his control over the American railroads, proclaiming him the "Modern Colossus of Roads."

Corbis/Library of Congress ©

While the Depot was a pleasant and inspiring place to be, the city to the north of it was not. Steam, smoke, and cinders poured from the departing and arriving locomotives, covering the northern Fourth Avenue area with black soot, vibrating motion, and the harsh clamor of deafening sounds. The Manhattan press conducted a full-throttle campaign, often with exaggerated reports of death and injury, in order to persuade the railroad company to develop a solution to the problem. A reporter for *Frank Leslie's Illustrated Newspaper* wrote in 1873, "Every few days there were accounts of the killing and wounding of persons about that frightful network of rails just beyond the depot." After an anti-railroad leaflet demanded the sinking of the tracks below ground level, the public demanded this as a solution. The city advised the railroad to sink its tracks below grade up to 96th Street, but the Vanderbilts resisted, having just spent $6,420,000 on the land and the construction of Grand Central Depot. The city persisted, however, and finally the Vanderbilts consented with the proviso that the city would provide half of the $6 million budget. In 1875, this was one of the earliest examples of collaboration between government and private industry. This public-private partnership would become increasingly popular at the end of the twentieth century and specifically at Grand Central.

By increasing the tracks from two to four lines, sinking them below street level, widening the avenue, and bridging the railroad with viaducts, an attractive urban thoroughfare was created. Smoke still spouted from the tracks below, but the din and vibrations were softened underground.

With each passing month, William H. Vanderbilt was assuming greater responsibility in the family business. In the winter of 1876, Cornelius became ill and died January 4, 1877, at the age of eighty-two. The father of thirteen children and numerous grandchildren through two marriages to distantly related cousins, Cornelius had created an empire that could rival the national economy. This centralizing of wealth gave him the power to alter the country's financial state at any time and was commented on with concern by leaders abroad. Great Britain's prime minister, William Gladstone, called Vanderbilt and his fortune "a danger to people at large," since one rash decision to sell off his stock could have crashed the market. Cornelius did not decentralize his wealth. He left his $94 million fortune and the business to William H., making him the wealthiest man in the country.

The Commodore's death was the end to one of history's most prolific industrial giants. William H. would no longer be dealing with the old-fashioned breed of captains of industry who chewed tobacco and kept accounts in their head. He was entering a world of educated, elitist moguls like J. P. Morgan. When William H. needed someone to advise him on how to control the seemingly uncontrollable finances of the railroad, he called on banking mogul J. P. Morgan. Morgan recommended the sale of 250,000 shares of New York Central stock—mostly to Great Britain to prevent a competing American line from acquiring the stock. The plan was a success; Morgan gained a seat on the board of directors and began his financial reign over the railroads.

In 1875, to reduce the number of accidents occurring at the on-grade crossings of Fourth Avenue (now Park Avenue), the New York Central and Hudson River Railroad lowered the tracks and connected the north- and southbound lanes of the thoroughfare with viaducts.

Courtesy of MTA/Metro-North Collection

William H. Vanderbilt relished the responsibility and continued to expand the family dynasty. The motto on the family's coat of arms, "Great Oaks Grow from Little Acorns," was about to become a reality. He began to acquire rail lines southwest of New York in Pennsylvania Railroad territory, spreading the company's rails as far as St. Louis. The move into the Pennsylvania region created a long-term battle between these two powerful companies; in response to this the Pennsylvania Railroad created a competing shore route that ran west of the Hudson River. Thus began a bidding war that had the potential to topple the American economy into a major economic depression.

J. P. Morgan saw the imminent danger to the economy and summoned the chief officers of the two companies to cruise with him on his luxurious yacht, *Corsair*. Steaming up and down the Hudson, they didn't stop until they came to an agreement that served both sides and steered the economy away from a free fall. The *Corsair* Agreement initiated a new era of railroad business, with Morgan as the new undisputed leader.

In 1883, William H. resigned as president and chairman of the New York Central but remained on the board to oversee operations. In 1885 he died from a burst blood vessel that occurred in the middle of a business argument. His older son, Cornelius Vanderbilt II, was named chairman, and the younger son, William K. Vanderbilt, was named chairman of constituent lines. This third generation of Vanderbilts involved in the railroad marked the beginning of the family's relinquishment of control of the business. By 1900, Cornelius

At the turn of the century, the congested rail yards just north of the station were a constant reminder to the railroad company that major improvements were overdue.

Vanderbilt II had died of a stroke and William K. renounced his executive responsibilities. Though the family retained major stock, and William K. remained an active member of the board, the company was no longer a Vanderbilt-operated railroad.

Nevertheless, the New York Central was building a name across the country and, as its headquarters, the Depot could not handle the large increase in passenger traffic. An ambitious public relations campaign for their new high-speed train, the Empire State Express, enhanced the railroad's image. From 1871 to the end of the nineteenth century, patronage increased over 400 percent, with 300 trains operating daily.

As *Railway Gazette* reported in December 1889, "The Grand Central yard is now one of the most crowded in the country. . . . The number of trains here are so great that even with a considerable amelioration of the conditions, the yard movements would still be very heavy. Engines are flying around in so many directions that injuries to employees are somewhat frequent, and no financial obstacles should stand in the way of the substantial abatement of the confusion now existing." Time was running out. Radical improvements were needed.

In 1898 the Depot underwent its first phase of renovations. Three floors were added to the head house, which raised the 42nd Street facade to 150 feet above street level. Bradford Gilbert, the architect for the renovation, chose the French Renaissance style for the remodeled Depot. The mansard roof towers were altered to classical tourelles except for the center tower of the 42nd Street facade, which was removed. The red brick exterior was refaced and a unified palette of materials, new fenestration, and an entrance pavilion created a classical treatment of clean lines. The building attained an elegance and sophistication that exceeded the original Depot. With all this came a new name, Grand Central Station.

As renovation plans continued to develop, Samuel Huckle, Jr., succeeded Gilbert as the project architect; he was joined by the new chief engineer of New

York Central, William J. Wilgus, whose genius would indelibly mark the railroad's future. Together they authored the second phase of renovations entailing major interior changes to the ground-floor passenger areas and the track system. By October of 1899, a construction process had begun that would not interfere with ongoing railroad operations. New tracks into the train shed were added and the entire system was reconfigured with a pneumatically powered interlocking system and switching devices to provide a safer and more efficient layout.

To accommodate the expanding number of passengers, every effort was made to improve the pedestrian flow through the building. Individual waiting rooms, originally built to serve the separate railroad lines, were combined into one great hall. Measuring 100 feet wide by 200 feet long with a 50-foot-high vaulted ceiling, this new feature was a prelude to the glorious Waiting Room of the Grand Central Terminal to come. Ticket counters were installed contiguous to the new waiting room.

As the final coat of paint was applied to the new Grand Central Station, the New York Central and Hudson River Railroad knew that its problem had not been solved. Overcrowding and safety still remained great concerns for chief engineer Wilgus as the twentieth century dawned. Wilgus, a man of great foresight, could see the railroad thriving in a new age of technology with the new

In 1899, architect Bradford Gilbert transformed the Depot into the Station by adding three stories and changing the building's style from the ornate French Empire to the classical Italianate.

Courtesy of MTA/Metro-North Collection

sources of electrical power at the core of the railroad's growth. Trains were continuing to flow with engines billowing smoke and the Station servicing traffic beyond its capacity despite the changes made during the renovation. As *Scientific American* commented in December 1900, "It is a remarkable fact that although New York is the second largest city in the world it has but one railroad terminal station within its boundaries. . . . The enormous volume of traffic which [Grand Central Station] has to accommodate has for many years proved too much for the capacity of the station yard."

A tragic accident became the catalyst for change when a disastrous rear collision occurred in the Fourth Avenue tunnel. At 8:20 A.M. on January 8, 1902, a New York Central commuter train heading for Grand Central on the Harlem line collided with a New Haven Line train in the Fourth Avenue tunnel at 54th Street. The New Haven train had stopped due to congestion in the train yard while the New York Central train had missed its signal to halt in the tunnel. Many passengers were killed or injured. The tracks at this point in the tunnel were often filled with smoke and steam, and on this particular day the conditions were exacerbated by the cold weather, making it more difficult for the trainmen to read the signals.

The public outcry for safer transportation made the New York Central even more aware of how serious the need was for a completely new facility. In December 1902, eleven months after the fatal train wreck, William Wilgus wrote a letter to New York Central president W. H. Newman, expressing his ideas for

One year after Bradford Gilbert completed his work on the Station, architect Samuel Huckle, Jr., revised the interior by combining three separate waiting rooms into one. This photograph, taken from the train shed in 1900, shows the extensive entrances into this grand room.

Courtesy of MTA/Metro-North Collection

With glass skylights between the beams of the roof, the destinations of the different lines inscribed above the doorways, and the classical decorative detail and overall immensity of space, the Grand Central Station waiting room was a preview of the future Terminal's Waiting Room.

Library of Congress, Prints and Photographs Division [LC-D4-17205]. Detroit Publishing Company Collection

a solution that was to become the foundation of the railroad's technological and real estate development: "air rights." In his letter, Wilgus stated, "the use of electricity dispenses with the necessity for the old style train sheds, and therefore with the use of new motive power. There is no reason why we should not utilize all of the valuable 'air' rights now covered by train sheds, aggregating over 200,000 square feet of surface."

By the end of 1902 the New York Central was committed to the electrification and construction of a new building. This novel stroke of real estate genius to generate income from land located above the tracks would not only solve the operational problems of the railroad and pay for the expensive electrification, but also change forever the heart of America's largest city. The real estate that would be created by depressing the railroad tracks would literally shape the modern skyscraper development of midtown Manhattan. The stage was set for the third and greatest railroad station to be built on 42nd Street: Grand Central Terminal.

CHAPTER THREE

HOW GRAND CENTRAL BECAME GRAND

Make no little plans; they have no magic to stir men's blood.
—DANIEL HUDSON BURNHAM

In 1899, when William Wilgus was chief engineer of the New York Central, he met an electric traction pioneer named Frank Sprague. Inspired by Sprague's ideas, Wilgus drew up an electrification plan for Grand Central Station that would create a new, multilevel terminal and also develop the real estate above the railroad tracks through the concept of "air rights." By the turn of the century, the need for such a plan was clear. The recently completed Grand Central Station's maximum capacity of 10 million passengers annually was, by the end of the twentieth century's first decade, exceeded by twice that number.

By March 1903 Wilgus had a solid plan for a 57-track, all-electric, double-level terminal on the desk of New York Central President William H. Newman. An entirely new terminal and office building would replace the old Grand Central Station, and hotels and other revenue-producing structures would be constructed on air rights above the terminal tracks. Starting at 56th Street, the four tracks that led down Park Avenue would be widened to ten tracks. A "throat" was formed to feed a double level of tracks submerged below street level. Loop tracks at both levels permitted trains to turn and quickly reassemble on outgoing tracks.

Steam locomotives had required open-air, vaulted spaces, but now, with electrified trams on underground tracks, Wilgus wrote that "from the air would be taken wealth with which to finance obligatory vast changes otherwise non-productive." Wilgus estimated that revenue-producing income from structures above the terminal tracks would produce an annual return of more than 3 percent, or $1,290,000 on the entire cost of the project. He was correct in his assessment. Ultimately the city blocks situated on top of this vast transportation complex were developed through Wilgus's air-rights concept and did have the kind of financial return he had hoped for.

Since the problems facing the New York Central Railroad and the Grand Central site could only be solved by completely rethinking the entire system of

The southwest corner of Grand Central Terminal a few months before its opening.
Avery Architectural and Fine Arts Library, Columbia University in the City of New York

William Wilgus, New York Central Railroad's chief engineer, was a visionary who brought travel and real estate development into the twentieth century.

Donald Duke Collection. Courtesy of William D. Middleton

train operations and passenger circulation, a station monumental in scale and design had to be constructed. This station would have to solve all rail operational problems as well as be of sufficient grandeur to become a centerpiece for the execution of the air-rights concept.

It was decided that an architectural competition should be held. In early 1903 four architectural firms were invited to participate from a pool of highly renowned designers and architects. Chicago's Daniel H. Burnham, of D. H. Burnham & Company, had designed New York's Flatiron building and Washington's Union Station. McKim, Mead & White of New York were single-handedly reshaping Manhattan and were the architects of many of New York's most important buildings, including New York's other monument to the railroad, Pennsylvania Station. Samuel Huckle, Jr., from Philadelphia had considerable transportation experience and worked with Wilgus on the 1900 interior renovation of Grand Central Station. The fourth firm, Reed & Stem, from St. Paul, Minnesota, was also experienced in station design, but far less well known. Charles Reed was connected to Wilgus through both design and family. At the time of the competition Reed had begun work with Wilgus on a new railroad station in Troy, New York, and his sister May was married to Wilgus.

The 1903 competition and the final selection of the architectural team to undertake the Terminal's grand design benefited from two significant steps in American architecture and civic design. The first began in the mid-nineteenth century when young aspiring American architects discovered the Ecole des Beaux Arts in Paris. The training at the Ecole was far superior to anything that was available in the United States at the time. Richard Morris Hunt, in 1850, began the exodus to Paris of young American architects who later became the leaders of the architectural profession back home in the United States after their study at the Ecole. This group included Daniel Burnham, Charles Follen McKim, Stanford White, Henry Hobson Richardson, Thomas Hastings, Louis Sullivan, Augustus Saint-Gaudens, Henry Ogden Avery, and Whitney Warren. Warren, although not one of the original four participants in the Grand Central competition, would later become principal author of the finished Terminal. All these men shared the brotherhood of being known as "Paris men," architects who studied the classical Greek and Roman orders of architecture, especially proportion, scale, and decorative composition, amid one of the world's greatest laboratories of architecture: Paris, the City of Light.

The second powerful influence on the ultimate design of Grand Central

Terminal was the emphasis that the Beaux Arts training placed on the connection between architecture and city planning, the emerging field of civic design. This influence was not solely Parisian; it was also very American. The 1893 Columbian Exposition in Chicago awakened architects to urban design and planning just as Frank Sprague had awakened Wilgus to electrification. Daniel Burnham, the exposition's chief architect, extolled the virtues of "an orderly and fitting arrangement of many buildings over the virtues of a single building," a statement that now seems amazingly prophetic of Grand Central's Terminal City and Wilgus's air-rights concept. The exposition evoked the City Beautiful movement in which grand American Renaissance palaces were constructed for the people. They included museums, libraries, opera houses, and universities. Buildings with grand spaces and lofty heights were being integrated into our urban fabric and into the architect's vocabulary.

It is regrettable that no record of Burnham's Grand Central competition entry survives, since it would have illustrated a powerful example of not only Beaux Arts design and details of the Terminal but also the ideas developed during the Columbian Exposition, and the approach to planning in relation to the surrounding city context. Nevertheless, the two surviving designs—McKim, Mead & White's and Reed & Stem's—contained bold city-planning scale ideas. In McKim's scheme, a sixty-story tower was placed on top of the Terminal and the crosstown streets and Park Avenue were allowed to run straight through the Terminal building.

Charles Reed's scheme created a design that expounded upon Wilgus's vision. It was an ambitious approach that combined a number of radical ideas into one package. Reed proposed an elevated roadway that ran around the circumference of the Terminal with sloping ramps seamlessly connecting its various levels. On the north side of the building he designed a vast "Court of Honor" above Park Avenue that would house the National Academy of Design and the Metropolitan Opera. The design's classical architecture and uniform building heights clearly showed the powerful influence of both Burnham and the Beaux Arts principles. Reed's plan also responded to Wilgus's remarkable concept of

THE GRAND CENTRAL TERMINAL STATION   NEW YORK CITY   FOR THE NEW YORK CENTRAL AND HUDSON RIVER·R·R·C°

In 1904, Warren & Wetmore joined
forces with Reed & Stem in the
design of Grand Central Terminal.
This drawing of the south facade
illustrates the Beaux Arts style that
Whitney Warren continued to develop for the building's final design.

the full electrification of the trains and station operations. In its scheme Reed
& Stem designed a brilliant way of moving vast numbers of people through the
Terminal by means of broad, sloping ramps, a design feature unlike any of the
other competition entries. This system of ramps effortlessly moved people to
and from platforms, a motion that was focused around Reed's central space,
the Main Concourse.

The Reed & Stem entry won the competition. If the losing architects
were left to wonder whether the decision was in any way influenced by the
connection of Reed and Wilgus by marriage, another family connection played
a significant role in the expansion of Reed & Stem's team. Whitney Warren, a
partner of the firm of Warren & Wetmore, was both a cousin and a close friend
of New York Central chairman William K. Vanderbilt. In 1904 Warren &
Wetmore were added to the architectural team at Vanderbilt's direction. Charles
Reed must have felt his David versus Goliath victory was a hollow one indeed.
Although the Reed & Stem/Warren & Wetmore association got off to a good
start, their ten-year battle of wills ended up in court.

A forced marriage of the two firms resulted in the formation of the
Associated Architects of Grand Central Terminal. Even though Charles Reed
was named chief executive of this new entity, Whitney Warren immediately
began to change Reed's original design concept. The plan for an office building
above the terminal was discarded. Stairs replaced ramps, and the design of the
waiting room and concourse was changed significantly. Warren's more formal
touches of Beaux Arts grandeur conformed with William K. Vanderbilt's ideas
of monumentality.

In the fall of 1906, while the architects were in the throes of designing
the new Terminal, the New York Central and the Hudson River Railroad operated the first electrified train into Grand Central Station. The new, electric-
driven locomotive passed through the 35-year-old curtain wall at the north end
of the train shed, a shed that by this time seemed to represent an outmoded

A 20-story office tower was planned to sit atop the Main Concourse. The Terminal's structural steel frame was constructed to support this tower. The plan was aborted in 1912, but the idea of an overbuild continued to linger until the landmarks victory in 1978.

Courtesy of MTA/Metro-North Collection

Whitney Warren's handwritten notes annotated the final design drawing for the 42nd Street facade.

Courtesy of MTA/Metro-North Collection

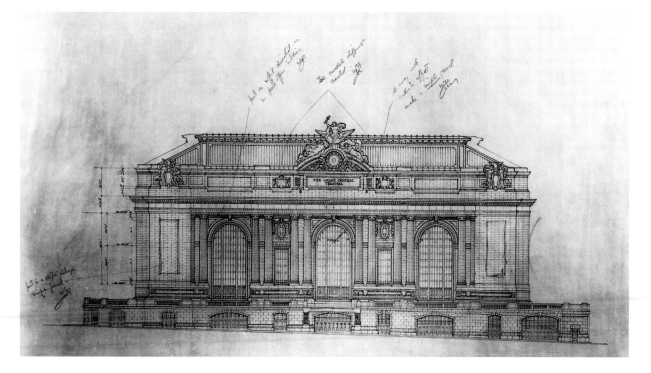

form of power. "Architectural fashions had changed almost as drastically as the
technology," wrote Carl Condit, "and Victorian intricacy hardly seemed appropriate to American Renaissance elegance and the gentle hum of electric motors."
The initial run was made by a special train including an office car, four coaches,
and three Pullmans drawn by locomotive #3406 with none other than William
Wilgus as the engineer.

The design of the Terminal proceeded; sometimes Warren's ideas prevailed and sometimes Reed's won the day. In 1907, only three days after the
opening of the railroad's new suburban electrification, Wilgus suddenly resigned.
With Wilgus gone and Warren fully in control of the design development of the
Terminal, Reed's ideas were spinning into oblivion. The New Haven Railroad,
which had final approval of design, however, soon rejected the Warren &
Wetmore design and had Charles Reed's work reincorporated, including the elevated roadway around the Terminal, the interior ramps, and a high-rise office
building above the Terminal concourse. The two firms had no alternative but
to find a way to work more closely together and they set about revising the
designs. By 1910, their jointly prepared drawings represented the building as it
was built over the next few years.

To prepare the site for the new Terminal, construction had begun in the

This view, looking south from the train yard in 1909, shows the Terminal under construction. As the Post Office (left, connected to the Terminal's office and baggage building) was nearing completion, the old Station's dome-capped towers are still visible on the right. Throughout a ten-year construction campaign, the New York Central and Hudson River Railroad continued service to and from New York City.

Courtesy of MTA/Metro-North Collection

summer of 1903. Between 42nd and 50th streets, over 200 buildings and structures were demolished and the site increased from 23 to almost 48 acres; 1.6 million cubic yards of rock and 1.2 million cubic yards of earth were excavated to make room for the yards and two levels of tracks and platforms; 29,000 tons of structural steel and one million barrels of cement went into the creation of the new Terminal. The steel frame alone required approximately 2.5 times the amount used to build the Eiffel Tower. All this construction was done while 800 trains and 75,000 people continued to flow through the existing station each day.

The excavation was made in three successive "bites," each completed before the next was undertaken, working westward from Lexington Avenue so that the traffic of the three railroads using the terminal continued. Before the demolition of the original station began, a temporary station on the Lexington Avenue side of the site was built. Dismantling the great iron train shed was a challenge: 1,700 tons of wrought iron, 150,000 square feet of roofing and glass, and more than half a million bricks had to be removed.

Grand Central was about to experience another turn of fate. Approximately fifteen months before the February 1913 opening of the new Terminal, Charles Reed died. Shortly after the funeral, Whitney Warren and his partner Charles Wetmore began legal proceedings for their firm to take over the entire project. Allen Stem was totally unaware of these proceedings, which nullified the Associated Architects agreement. The remainder of the project was solely in the hands of Warren & Wetmore. When the building was complete, a decade after it began construction, only one firm's name, Warren & Wetmore, was publicly recognized as the building's architect. Reed's surviving partner, Allen Stem, sued for Reed & Stem's fair share of the fees jointly earned by both firms. Years passed before the legal case was settled; Warren & Wetmore eventually paid Stem & Reed's estate close to half a million dollars.

As often happens in creative partnerships, the darker side of human nature is not necessarily reflected in the final product. Both Warren and Reed made equally important contributions to the building's unique design. As historians of Grand Central have noted on numerous occasions, it would not have become such a fine building if it had come from the hand of only one of these two very talented, strong-willed architects.

29,000 tons of steel form the structure for the Terminal and the planned office tower above. The steel frame construction marked a turning point in American architecture; high-rise buildings no longer had to be formed by load-bearing masonry walls.

Courtesy of MTA/Metro-North Collection

"A Glory of the Metropolis," declared a *New York Times* editorial when Grand Central Terminal officially opened at midnight on February 1, 1913. During the afternoon and evening of February 1, guests of the architects, numbering up to 2,000, took a tour of the Terminal. When the doors opened at midnight to a cheering public, 3,000 people rushed into the building in awe of its grandeur and volume. *Scientific American* called Grand Central Terminal "a monumental gateway to America's greatest city." The first train left the terminal at 12:25 A.M. February 2. "Its beauty," the *Times* stated, "is chiefly that of mass and line and color, all simple and all, because of that quality, the more effective and impressive."

The *Times*'s editorialist had certainly captured one of the Terminal's significant characteristics: its quiet but powerful presence at the newly important intersection of Park Avenue and East 42nd Street. Overnight, the south facade with its three arched windows—each one 33 feet wide and 60 feet high, enframed in Stony Creek granite and Bedford limestone—gave the city a new entry portal, a modern-day version of an historic triumphal arch.

The composition of the facade, with these three great portals, was crowned by an immense sculptural group above 42nd Street some 60 feet wide, 50 feet high, and weighing 1,500 tons. Jules-Alexis Coutan's sculpture of Mercury supported by Hercules (moral energy) on one side and Minerva (mental energy) on the other side, and crowned with the spreading wings of a giant eagle, was soon a much-admired New York landmark, "the best piece of monumental sculpture in America," extolled the classicist Henry Hope Reed, Jr.

Behind this imposing street presence, the Terminal's interior spaces expressed their huge scale through a simplicity of mass, line, and color. In the center of the building, one great space became the focal point for all long-distance departures. This space, the Main Concourse, was 275 feet long, 120 feet wide, and 125 feet high, framed at its eastern and western ends by 90-foot-high double-glazed walls with glass-floored walkways between them. The ceiling of this great space was an astrological mural depicting an artistic version of the constellation, as envisioned from above. Conceived by Warren and his friend, the French portraitist Paul Helleu, the mural was the creation of J. Monroe Hewlett and Charles Basing. Corps of astronomers and painting assistants worked with Hewlett and Basing. Some 2,500 stars were painted onto a cerulean blue sky ceiling; 60 of these stars were illuminated in varying degrees of light levels. Along the north and south sides of this ceiling, five clerestory windows were set into the curved night sky. The effect was to bring the heavens inside the building.

As New Yorkers absorbed the beauty and monumentality of this wonderful new building, it became apparent that it worked brilliantly as a railroad station as well. Or, more precisely, as *three* railroad stations. The awe-inspiring Beaux Arts architecture was actually an elegant setting for a breakthrough in railroad station planning and real estate development. The architects developed a plan that located three separate stations on two levels. On the upper level on the western side of the Terminal, the incoming tracks were built with passenger facilities—including baggage handling, cab driveways, passages leading directly to subways, adjoining buildings and the street, and spaces to receive and greet arriving long-distance passengers. This was quite separate and set apart from the facilities to serve departing long-distance passengers. The departing long-distance trains were located on the same level

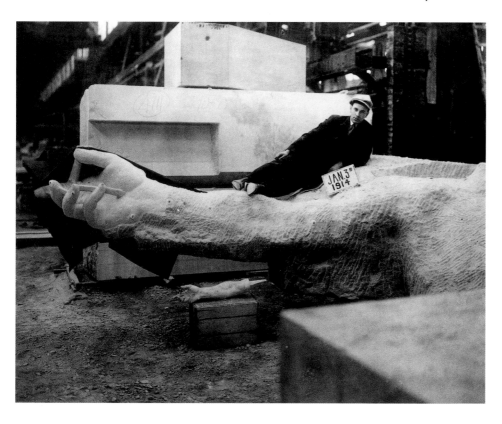

To illustrate the immense size of the Terminal's sculpture, a craftsman poses on the arm of Mercury. Below is the plaster model that guided sculptor Alexis Coutan.

Courtesy of Building Stone Institute

In 1914, the massive sculpture group has been set on top of the 42nd Street facade, the stores are in business, and the viaduct linking the circumferential drive to Park Avenue is nearing completion. Grand Central Terminal has claimed the corner of 42nd Street and Vanderbilt Avenue.

Courtesy of MTA/Metro-North Collection

Located off the main Waiting Room were smaller, separate spaces for men and women. The Ladies Waiting Room and Bathroom shown here was lined with oak paneling, marble encasements, and decorative plaster relief. Notice the rocking chairs for nursing mothers.

Avery Architectural and Fine Arts Library, Columbia University in the City of New York

The Waiting Room, one of the city's most stately public spaces, was designed to serve travelers, who often spent hours waiting for connecting trains. They could relax on the oak benches surrounded by fresh greenery in an environment of warmth and grandeur.

Courtesy of MTA/Metro-North Collection

Photographed just after the Terminal opened, the Oyster Bar ramps combine the elegance of Warren's Beaux Arts detail with Reed's free-flowing circulation.

Courtesy of MTA/Metro-North Collection

but in the center and easterly portion of the new Terminal, and the area included facilities that departing passengers needed at the commencement of their journey: ticketing, baggage checking, track information, and stores for last-minute shopping. One level below was the third station serving the ever-growing suburban traffic with its own ticketing, waiting, and information facilities. Travelers flowed through the Terminal using a series of generous and gently sloping ramps, linking together each part of the building while at the same time skillfully separating the growing numbers of incoming, outgoing, and suburban traffic. The ease of pedestrian flow through the Terminal was also aided by a minimum of baggage, mail, and parcels movement at the train platform level. A series of subway passages, some 50 to 60 feet below street level, was used for this purpose and was connected to all the platforms above by special freight elevators.

The number of people using the Terminal continued to be astonishing, as the entire country seemed to be turning into an itinerant society. At the commencement of construction in 1903, daily train traffic stood at 44,200. By 1919 it had doubled to 88,500, and to 111,040 daily riders by 1921. The Terminal's seemingly limitless capacity is the result not only of the superb pedestrian spaces but also of the railroad engineering technology that designed and built two loop tracks to serve the upper and suburban levels of tracks. Using the loop tracks, incoming trains enter on the western side of the Terminal and, after discharging passengers, run around the loop to the eastern or midpoint platforms to pick up

This 1913 view of the Main Concourse just after its completion shows the space in its purest state. Electricity, a new technology, gives the monumental space an even glow of illumination.

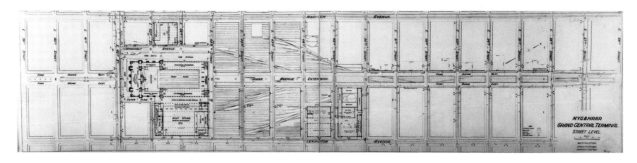

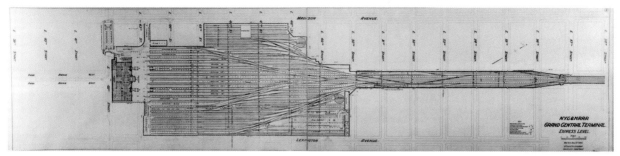

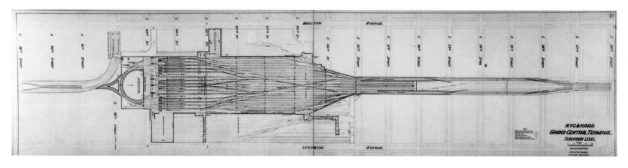

The plans of the three different levels of track layout demonstrate the enormous capacity of train traffic the Terminal was designed to accommodate.

Courtesy of MTA/Metro-North Collection

departing passengers. This greatly increases the traffic capacity of the Terminal.

Along with the creation of a new passenger terminal, 32 miles of electrified tracks on two underground levels were constructed on 40 acres of land between 42nd and 53rd streets. This land would eventually be developed for hotels, office buildings, apartments, clubs, and retail stores, using the air-rights concept as a way to pay the extremely high costs of electrifying the railroad's operations. This was the other aspect of Wilgus's brilliant concept, the real estate component that would literally shape the heart of New York City.

For Grand Central Terminal, it is clearly the combination of architectural elegance and engineering genius that created together what could not have been done alone. As Douglas Haskell reflected in *Architectural Forum* fifty years after the building's creation, "The brilliant breakthrough of Grand Central Terminal came from the fact that during the first decade of our century, New York brought together her two major achievements—concentrated building and swift urban transportation—into a single inter-related planned operation. The event was majestically fantastic. It stood at the pinnacle of creative effort . . . the great movement of urban 'futurism.' "

42 ST LOOKING WEST FROM GRAND CENTRAL

04

CHAPTER FOUR

REAL ESTATE AND TRAIN TRAVEL

. . . more than a gateway, more than a terminal, the terminal proper, the great head house and its accompanying buildings are simply the heart and the cause of a group of buildings that has best been described as a "terminal city."
—*NEW YORK TIMES*, FEBRUARY 2, 1913

Within a decade of its opening, Grand Central Terminal was at the center of intense high-rise development. This, coupled with the great range of services within the Terminal, made the area seem as though it were a city within a city. Wilgus's original vision of air-rights development had resulted in a constant and huge flow of people that extended beyond the terminal walls via its many approaches, passages, and ramps to neighboring sites, which were now being intensively developed by the railroad. New York Central was becoming not only a state-of-the-art railroad shaping the travel habits of the nation but also a mega-developer of the new business district that was changing the face of New York City.

By 1913 when Grand Central Terminal officially opened its doors to the public, half of the air-rights sites had been either built upon or planned for future construction. Sites that were once considered locations of a last resort were now very valuable real estate.

Before the Terminal's completion, the first wave of buildings were not the most distinguished architecturally, as the railroad company focused on building hotels to provide overnight accommodations for the thousands of travelers who needed a place to stay between trips. In 1887 the Vanderbilts had constructed the Railroadmen's YMCA, known as "Old 361," on Madison Avenue and 45th Street —which subsequently became the site of the Roosevelt Hotel. This was followed by hotels such as the Manhattan (1901), the Belmont (1906), and the Vanderbilt (1911), forerunners of a new type of hotel design that emphasized size, convenience, and a somewhat cold commercial approach in their vast public rooms. Prior to this era, hotels had been more of an extension of the domestic world— smaller, more elegant, and reflective of the personality of their resident owners.

By 1920, 42nd Street, one of Manhattan's major crosstown thoroughfares, was lined with a motion that never ceased.

Corbis/Library of Congress ©

Following the Terminal's completion, four hotels that set the standard
for modern comforts and luxurious surroundings were the Biltmore, located on
the block between Madison and Vanderbilt avenues, 43rd to 44th streets (1914,
Warren & Wetmore, architects); the Commodore, located on 42nd Street
between Lexington Avenue and Grand Central Terminal (1919, Warren &
Wetmore, architects); the Ambassador on Park Avenue between 51st and 52nd
streets—the northernmost limit of the New York Central's air-rights district
(1921, Warren & Wetmore, architects); and the Waldorf-Astoria, between Park
and Lexington avenues and 49th and 50th streets (1931, Schultze & Weaver,
architects). Together, they provided over 5,000 guest rooms and great public
rooms—ballrooms, dining rooms, atriums, lounges, restaurants—that were pala-
tial in their scale and glamorous in their finishing and furnishings. Each of them
served a different type of clientele. The Commodore and the Biltmore appealed
to commercial and business trade, while the Ambassador and Waldorf-Astoria
offered the refined elegance of the great European hotels. Built in a classical and
decorative architectural style, these hotels brought great sophistication to the
New York street scene.

The competition for guests became fierce. Brochures boasting Grand
Central as the "Gateway to a Continent" advertised the fact that eight of the

The Railroad Y.M.C.A. was used for overnight stays by railroad employees. Located on Park Avenue between 49th and 50th streets, it was later moved to 224 East 47th Street to make room for the Waldorf-Astoria. To the right is one of the towers of the power plant that supplied electricity to the Grand Central district. To the left is St. Bartholomew's Church.

Courtesy of MTA/Metro-North Collection

In 1929, the block between 49th and 50th streets on the east side of Park Avenue was developed as the new Waldorf-Astoria, designed by Schultze & Weaver. With its numerous linkages to Grand Central, the Waldorf was a prime example of the Terminal City concept.

Corbis/Library of Congress ©

HOTEL ROOSEVELT
Madison to Vanderbilt Avenues—45th to 46th Streets
Early American atmosphere in decorations and furnishings; 1100 spacious, attractive guest rooms; air-conditioned public rooms; private passageway direct to Grand Central Terminal.

B. G. HINES
Managing Director

A promotional rendering of the Roosevelt, one of the new breed of midtown Manhattan hotels built as a result of the excitement and glamour of rail travel.

from *The Gateway to a Continent.* Courtesy of William D. Middleton

world's best-known hotels were within walking distance, several of which were on Park Avenue. The Hotel Commodore was located right next to Grand Central with an express subway heading to all parts of the city from the lower lobby. The Hotel Biltmore was located directly above the Terminal's arrival tracks, so that it was possible for a person to book a room at the Biltmore, arrive at Grand Central, and take an elevator from the concourse level or walk up a short flight of stairs from the Incoming Station Waiting Room to the hotel lobby without going outside. In the 1940s a honeymooning couple had arrived at the Terminal to take a train to Niagara Falls when a violent storm struck the city, disrupting all service. The couple took a room in the Biltmore, had their meals at the Oyster Bar, shopped in the Terminal's stores, and spent the weekend without once venturing out into the hostile weather.

The Hotel Roosevelt, spanning 45th to 46th streets between Madison and Vanderbilt, had more than 1,100 spacious rooms and a private passageway that led directly into Grand Central. Nearby, but not as intimately connected to the Terminal, were the Barclay and Park Lane. A popular advertisement at that time read: "Uncrowded seclusion, hidden away from the hurly burly of the city, for those who demand the extra relaxation of such quiet havens. . . . Whatever the human whim for its sojourn in New York, it will find adequate answer in one of the distinctive hotels conveniently located near Grand Central Terminal."

Terminal City's extremely rapid block-by-block growth of hotels, offices, and apartment buildings was accomplished in part because New York Central's overall planning had included the construction of a massive power and heating plant at Park Avenue between 49th and 50th streets. This plant served the railroad facilities as well as the entire air-rights district. But by the 1920s, New York's power supply was being taken over by the utility companies, and so the valuable real estate on which the plant had stood was developed for a greater investment return. In 1929, construction of the Waldorf-Astoria began on this site with its own secret underground track connection from Grand Central to a train platform beneath the hotel. Also within this underground facility was a "garage" for private railroad cars. A midblock driveway connecting 49th and 50th streets was constructed wide enough to accommodate a Rolls-Royce or a limousine. After Franklin D. Roosevelt's 1944 presidential campaign speech at the Waldorf, he descended to track 61 and caught the presidential train back to Hyde Park without ever leaving the building. One of Grand Central's best-kept secrets, this passageway was used in 1965 for one of Andy Warhol's "underground parties."

As midtown Manhattan continued to grow and rival the city's traditional downtown financial and business district, office buildings began to rise around the Terminal. The Park-Lexington by Warren & Wetmore (1922–23) on Park Avenue between 4th and 47th streets was a twenty-story steel-frame office complex that covered an entire city block. Other new office buildings began to fill the land surrounding the Terminal. The Graybar Building (1927) was the first Art Deco building in the Grand Central zone. Located on Lexington Avenue

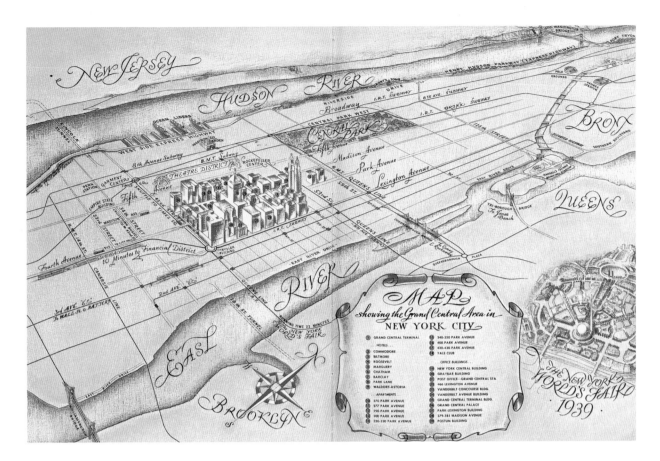

A map highlighting the position of
the Grand Central area in relation to
Manhattan's primary geography.

from *The Gateway to a Continent.* Courtesy
of William D. Middleton

This Warren & Wetmore drawing of
the New York Central Building illustrates the concept of air rights as well
as the continuous flow of Park
Avenue.

Courtesy of MTA/Metro-North Collection

between 43rd and 44th streets, the Graybar was one block north of the Commodore with an arcade leading directly into the Terminal, which decades later became known as the Graybar Passage. Its creamy travertine-lined walls, vaulted plaster ceiling, and terrazzo floor comprised an interior design treatment deliberately in sympathy with the Terminal's interior finishes. Other distinguished neighbors included the Chanin Building (1929), the Art Deco Chrysler Building (1930), and the Daily News Building (1930). Clubs to serve the new business elite like the Yale Club (1912), the New York Yacht Club (1903), and the University Club (1900) all became an important part of the midtown scene.

The high-rise growth around Grand Central allowed American architects to demonstrate their prowess in the new field of designing skyscrapers. The New York Central Building (1929), headquarters of the New York Central Railroad Company, was Warren & Wetmore's opportunity to design a 35-story needle-like tower closing the Park Avenue vista at 46th Street. Immediately to the north of Grand Central Terminal, spanning 45th and 46th streets, and embracing the northbound and southbound roadway of Park Avenue, the tower was a bold

An aerial photo of Park Avenue, showing how William Wilgus's concept of air rights had developed by the 1930s to become a glamorous city above the railroad tracks.

from *The Gateway to a Continent.* Courtesy of William D. Middleton

urban design, illustrating the integration of structure and movement in one built form. It was a more modest but effective interpretation of the monumental Court of Honor that Charles Reed had designed as part of his winning Grand Central competition entry in 1903. Known today as the Helmsley Building, and now with the addition of a garishly gilded roof, it continues to dominate the Park Avenue vista despite the overpowering presence behind it of the MetLife fifty-five-story tower, formerly the Pan Am Building, constructed in 1963.

This 1912 *Scientific American* cover by Jules Guerin dramatically illustrates that the new Grand Central is the city's gateway. Large crowds converge on the Terminal at the street and elevated roadway levels.

Avery Architectural and Fine Arts Library, Columbia University in the City of New York

Between 1920 and 1930, Park Avenue was rapidly expanding northward outside the Grand Central zone as far uptown as 96th Street. And though much of the railroad's air rights were used for luxurious hotels and office buildings, new luxury apartment buildings and town houses were also being built, as Park Avenue became a very desirable residential address. One beautiful exception to all this commercial and speculative development was Bertram Goodhue's St. Bartholomew's Church (1917–23), on Park Avenue at 51st Street. Rich in the splendorous style of Byzantine architecture, which Goodhue greatly admired, the church's triple arched portal leading out to Park Avenue was designed by Stanford White. Its bronze doors bear the legend "to the Glory of God and in loving memory of Cornelius Vanderbilt."

Once considered much too far uptown, 42nd Street was no longer the northern frontier of Manhattan's growth. It had become an important crosstown street. A few blocks to the west of the Terminal, the city's fledgling entertainment district was growing around Times Square, and new retail development had begun to extend along 42nd Street between Grand Central and Fifth Avenue. The city was alive with mass movement and ablaze at night with that magical new invention, electricity, a twentieth-century technology that not only powered the new generation of trains but also brought the city to life twenty-four hours a day.

Like an iceberg, Grand Central revealed only a part of its bulk above the surface. Beneath Park Avenue were 79 acres of tracks and switches. People strolling along the avenue would often hear sounds, albeit muffled, of electric locomotive bells directly under their feet. After the completion of the Lexington

Avenue IRT subway system, the Terminal's underground grew even more extensive. "Chief strands in this vast network," noted Carl Condit, "constitute a continuous underground rail and subway system that is . . . tied to the street above and to the vertical transportation provided by the elevators in high-rise buildings. It is a staggering urban phenomenon, and not even the Circle Line of the London Underground, which unites the city's 16 railroad terminals in a complete circuit, can show anything remotely comparable to it."

Terminal City, Grand Central Terminal and its surrounding development greatly exceeded even Wilgus's expectations. Unlike its predecessors—the Depot and the Station—Grand Central Terminal would withstand the demands of time. But neither Vanderbilt nor Wilgus could have known that it would become not only the cornerstone for New York's development but also the gateway to the continent during the golden age of train travel.

Rail travel was becoming increasingly popular. The burgeoning population was moving around the country in ever-growing numbers at ever increasing speeds. In 1903, the year that planning for the Terminal began, the old Grand Central was already handling over 50,000 passengers each work day—over 16 million each year. As

One of the components of Terminal City, the Hotel Commodore faces 42nd Street and is connected to Grand Central by an entrance below the circumferential drive on the left.
Courtesy of MTA/Metro-North Collection

travel became an everyday activity for a growing majority of the urban population, greater emphasis was placed on safety, speed, and comfort. Through electrification, illuminated signalization, more powerful locomotives, steel cars, and greater passenger amenities were now possible. In 1893 the Exposition Flyer was the first high-speed train between New York and Chicago, traveling at speeds up to 90 miles per hour. After arriving in Chicago, it was proudly displayed by the New York Central at the 1893 Columbian Exposition. George H. Daniels, the New York Central's senior passenger agent and public relations officer, one of the industry's most enterprising employees, conceived the idea of an even faster and more luxurious train. Daniels named it the Twentieth Century when it started daily service in 1902, adding Limited to its name a short time later when its number of stops was reduced. Taking advantage of these new technologies, it

traveled the 960 miles between New York and Chicago in twenty hours. A great fleet of such trains crisscrossed the nation. Known as the Limiteds, they had evocative names: the Empire State, the Wolverine, the Commodore Vanderbilt, Pacemaker, Lake Shore, the Yankee Clipper, the Southwestern, and the most famous of all, the Twentieth Century Limited, known to its habitués simply as the Century.

The Century grew to symbolize everything that was exciting, adventurous, and glamorous about rail travel. Its amenities were developed to serve the growing sophistication of the traveling public with comfortable seating, separate dining and sleeping cars, roomettes, barber and beauty salons, secretarial services, and telephone and telegraph services. By the 1920s the Century was an all-steel 14-car train pulled by new, powerful locomotives. Known as Hudsons (after their route), these locomotives were capable of sustaining high speeds for long stretches. The Limited's popularity grew throughout the halcyon decade of the 1920s, to the point that on December 3, 1928, the Century's westbound train number 25 carried a total of 800 passengers in seven sections (railroad nomenclature for seven separate trains). A month later on January 7, 1929, this record was outdone by eastbound train number 26 which had 822 passengers. But perhaps the most impressive fact about these journeys was that all seven separate trains arrived before or on time.

In 1938, a new Twentieth Century Limited with increased comfort and speed was designed by Henry Dreyfuss, the nation's most famous industrial designer. It had a sleeker look with an Art Moderne motif throughout its interior and exterior, and a distinctive tail sign illuminated by a blue fluorescent bulb. The trusty and swift Hudson locomotives were given redesigned, streamlined, bullet-nose cowlings for the engine. While the new design of the train and what the train represented captivated passengers, an advertising campaign as alluring as the train itself followed. "Your arrival is an event! And your trip on board the

'Century' truly an Overnight Vacation." Fresh sole and strawberries for breakfast, a newspaper delivered by your door and boutonnieres upon entering the dining cars. These extravagances were underscored by ads showing happy couples arriving at their destination like celebrities, surrounded by waiting crowds and spectators. "No other train in the world makes a night of travel such a memorable experience. Strain vanishes the instant you enter your accommodations—private, of course." All this was underscored by ads with the slogan "It Saves a Day."

Boarding the Century was an event in itself. A redcap would take you and your baggage to the Twentieth Century gate. After a conductor checked your ticket, you walked toward the train on a long, deep crimson red carpet with the words "Twentieth Century Limited" in silver-gray lettering. It was the Art Moderne version of the yellow brick road. The daily roll-out of the red carpet for the arrival and departure of the Century increased the allure and mystique of Grand Central Terminal and the trains that arrived and departed from it.

Just as a passenger in the 1990s flying the Concorde to London or Paris would expect to travel with the Who's Who of the business, entertainment, and social worlds, the passenger list of a typical Century bristled with the names of the rich and famous, such as Gloria Swanson, Fred Astaire, Ginger Rogers, Cary Grant, and Greta Garbo. Greta Garbo, in her desire for solitude and in order not to be mobbed by crowds of fans, would take an elevator from the train to the baggage room and disappear unseen into a taxi. Oswald S. Thorne, a redcap at Grand Central in 1940 told readers in *The Railroaders Magazine* that Jimmy Durante always had a ten-dollar bill in his hand no matter how many bags he possessed. Joan Crawford and Marlene Dietrich always needed two or three redcaps and were always good tippers. Mae West traveled with an entourage of six men who took care of the redcaps. John D. Rockefeller, no matter how many bags he had, would look a redcap straight in the eye and give him a dime.

The early-morning arrival of the eastbound Twentieth Century Limited drew hundreds of celebrity hunters poised against rope barriers "like duck hunters waiting in their blinds," according to a *New York Times* reporter in 1939.

Redcaps roll out the red carpet for the Century's passengers. Arrivals and departures were always met with fanfare.
Penn Central Company. Courtesy of William D. Middleton

In 1948, General Dwight D. Eisenhower (not yet president), actress Beatrice Lillie, and Mayor William O'Dwyer christen the new, postwar Century with a bottle of water from the Mohawk and Hudson Rivers and the Great Lakes.
© NYT Pictures

A Twentieth Century Limited menu from the 1940s.

Talented chefs and kitchen crews of the Twentieth Century Limited created such delicious selections as lobster bisque, filet mignon, and crème caramel with unbelievable efficiency in limited quarters.

Courtesy of MTA/Metro-North Collection

The Century's habitués gather in the dining car to pass the travel time with a gourmet meal.

Courtesy of MTA/Metro-North Collection

Though the Terminal's stationmaster tried to keep the volume of people down by not announcing the arrival track until the last minute or by posting it on a blackboard in a waiting room at the west end of the station, it did not restrain regular visitors to the Century. They knew the pattern of probable tracks for the train's arrival and spread the word to those who were newer at the game.

The New York Central's great rival, the Pennsylvania Railroad, which operated across town at Pennsylvania Station on 34th Street, had its own fleet of Limiteds including the Broadway Limited, which rivaled the Century. But they competed for prestige, not profit. The truth was that the Limiteds were not moneymakers for either company but enhanced the railroad's image to the public and were a good source of advertising. Thus both railroads agreed to the same running time of their competing trains between Chicago and New York, which clocked in at twenty hours in 1920, eighteen hours in 1932, and sixteen and one-half hours in 1935.

The number of rail passengers continued to climb during the 1920s, reaching 145,600 passengers a day in 1929. Although weekend traffic usually was not high, there was a memorable Saturday on November 25, 1916, when 129,486 passengers used the Terminal on their journeys to and from the Yale/Harvard football game. In the sixteen years since its opening in 1913, the Terminal's annual traffic increased from 23 million to almost 47 million passengers. With all the amenities of a city within a city, Grand Central was in these optimistic times the focus of the surrounding growth of a great modern city, an unsurpassed network of communication, and a symbol of people's hopes and dreams.

CHAPTER FIVE

HOME TO THE NATION

Every night when I go home from my job I'm sure I've seen everything. Next day back at work I know I haven't. . . . You understand what a visiting maharaja meant when he said: "Why this is not a railroad station. This is a temple for all people."
—STATIONMASTER EDWARD FISCHER, *COLLIERS* MAGAZINE, MARCH 5, 1954

When the familiar fabric of American life began to unravel with the stock market crash of 1929 and the subsequent bank failures of the 1930s, Grand Central Terminal remained a place that symbolized better times and a home away from home for many people. While the railroads reported a sharp increase in people who roamed the country in empty boxcars, a small community was forming on the North Balcony within the Terminal. Referred to by many as the "professors," they met regularly, shared words and cigarettes, contemplated life, and observed human behavior. It was a place from which they could not be evicted or foreclosed. Named the "Philosophers' Gallery," the balcony community's reputation grew within the Terminal and attracted many of the rail workers. On any given day, the unemployed—many of whom had been poor before the crash and others who had once been flush enough to ride the Twentieth Century Limited—were joined by veteran railroaders. In 1931, the "professors" had to share their space on the North Balcony with a twelve-foot, one-ton model of the Cathedral of Saint John the Divine, which was on display to raise enough funds to build the cathedral. This gave people in the space the feeling of sitting on an aisle in church overlooking a rather eclectic congregation.

While President Hoover was in the White House conferring with business leaders who were creating schemes for "industrial self-government," smaller steps were being taken in Grand Central that didn't create employment but maintained a level of dignity and normalcy for those hardest hit by the Depression. A charitable organization, the United Neighborhood Houses, began a long-term arrangement with the National Plant, Fruit and Flower Guild in Grand Central asking people who commuted to New York from the suburbs to bring in flowers for the thousands of poorer city dwellers who could no longer afford them.

The quintessential Grand Central photograph taken in the 1930s shows sunlight streaming through the lunette windows onto the marble floor below, making the Main Concourse a space of calm grandeur.
Courtesy of MTA/Metro-North Collection

Stationmaster Edward Fischer stands
on duty in the 1950s, maintaining
order in a place where anything
could happen.
© Werner Wolff/Black Star

The calming, soothing presence of floral arrangements in the summer
and fall was followed by musical programs starting at Thanksgiving, continuing
through Christmas and the New Year, and returning in time for Easter, courtesy
of the railroad. During the Christmas season the sights and smells of huge
Christmas trees, ornamented with 500 lights each, and a twenty-foot diameter
wreath were accompanied by songs of the season, filling the Terminal with
memories of home. One Easter, travelers were serenaded by members of the
Manhattan Concert Band, composed of WPA employees as part of FDR's New
Deal. This musical tradition continued through the Depression and World War
II and was anchored by one woman, Mrs. Mary Lee Read. She started playing
in Grand Central in 1928 on an organ borrowed from a department store. When
she first arrived in the Terminal, she bowed her head in prayer, asking God
to allow her to be the one to put music into the space. She promised that if it
happened, she would devote her life to this work and to this place—which she
ultimately did.

Many artists found help and inspiration at Grand Central Terminal. "I'm
a playwright in need of inspiration," said this traveler. "I do my best thinking
when I'm riding on a train. I have about ten bucks to spend on inspiration.
Where do I go?" The clerk sold him a round-trip ticket to Albany.

It was during this period that Grand Central had its own version of "selling the Brooklyn Bridge." After searching New York for the perfect site to open
their business, the Fortunato brothers handed over a certified check for $10,000
to a couple of confidence tricksters in the belief that they could set up a fruit
stand in the information booth's central location in the Main Concourse. Imagine
Nick and Tony Fortunato's shock when they arrived the day after the deal with
tools, lumber, and carpenters ready to begin construction. Police from the in-
house police station stopped them and their hopes for fame and fortune. The
hustlers were never found. In all probability they took the Fortunato brothers'
$10,000 and left town by rail.

The building had its share of "freelance businesspeople" who knew how
to make a fast buck in any economic climate. Referred to by the workers of the
Lost and Found as "car walkers," they waited until an incoming train was almost
empty and then walked through the cars scouting for articles left behind by
other passengers. If assessments by the clerks in the Lost and Found department
are any judge, these car walkers did quite well: wallets, umbrellas, coats, jewelry.
Strange finds like false teeth, glass eyes, or artificial arms left workers trying to
figure out how owners were managing without a missing body part or chewing
a meal without teeth and why they never called for their items. Whatever wasn't
stolen or remained unclaimed in the Lost and Found was, in these difficult
times, donated to charity.

Every day during the 1920s and 1930s there were steady streams of men,
women, and children asking to claim something that they had supposedly lost.
But even under the most dire of economic circumstances human behavior at the
Lost and Found could be poignant or even entertaining. Once a woman came

to the window looking for her husband. The clerk told her that normally missing people didn't turn themselves into the Lost and Found. He had just suggested the stationmaster's office when she screamed, "There he is!" pointing to a small glass urn on the shelf. The clerk asked her to identify the contents, as he did for any claim, and she explained that on her way home from the crematorium she had accidentally left him on the train seat next to hers. As the woman turned away from the window with her urn, the attendant heard her say to the jar, "Let's go home, dear, it's all over now."

Long before Franklin D. Roosevelt advocated a New Deal for America's "forgotten man," Grand Central Terminal was a democratic space in which the man or woman on the street could feel extraordinary, despite the anonymity and sheer numbers of the crowd. A letter written by Esther Levy, a worker in the Graybar Building, and published in the *Grand Central Zone Tab* in February 1929, reflects the feeling.

The North Balcony offered a place for contemplation, conversation, and observation of the bustle below where a million lives were constantly intersecting.

Courtesy of MTA/Metro-North Collection

Dear Sir:

You may think me overemotional but I want to draw the attention of the workers in and about Grand Central to the very great beauty of that terminal. I am a worker in the Graybar building, and I never cut across the wide marble expanse of Grand Central into my own particular corridor without breathing a little prayer of thanksgiving that I am privileged to work amidst such grandeur and beauty. If Grand Central were located in ancient Greece or Rome, we'd be frantically saving up our pennies so that we could go to see it. When I leave my office, a little after 5, and walk across Grand Central to the shuttle entrance, I am thrilled and uplifted at the powdery blue twilight that fills the vast upper spaces of the marble palace which is our station. The crowds, the lights, the varied noises, all blending in the greatness of the place to the minor notes of a city symphony —all of these give me a gift of beauty for which I never cease, even in the horrors of my subway jam, to be grateful.

After the Depression Grand Central started blossoming again. A feeling of rejuvenation filled the Terminal as bustling commuters went back to work. In 1936 construction work began on a 242-seat newsreel theater with entrances from Grand Central and the Graybar Building. A rail history museum, free to the public, opened in 1940 and exhibited more than a century of the history of

American railroads. Long-distance travel increased during this period, resulting in the expansion of Grand Central's information services. In July 1941, two travel bureaus were opened in the Terminal. Located just off the Main Waiting Room they had red leather armchairs, cabinets of travel folders, and agents to arrange itineraries.

This period of optimism and rejuvenation was short-lived. On December 7, 1941, Japanese forces attacked Pearl Harbor and the United States went to war. Grand Central, gateway to a continent, became a place where soldiers began and ended their journeys to places well beyond America's soil. A pallor fell over the Terminal the day America went to war. Mary Read, in an effort to raise the spirits of the commuters, played "The Star Spangled Banner" during rush hour and brought the entire Main Concourse to a complete standstill. The stationmaster asked Read not to play anything that would keep commuters from reaching their trains on time. She gained the reputation of being the only organist in New York forbidden to play "The Star-Spangled Banner."

Mary Lee Read seated at her organ on Grand Central's balcony.
Collection of New York Central System Historical Society Inc.

A choir sings holiday classics from the North Balcony.
© NYT Pictures

After Pearl Harbor the men in the Philosophers' Gallery disappeared. Perhaps they got jobs or were sent to war. But they were not the only men missing from Grand Central. Workers in the Terminal had ranged in age from twenty to sixty-seven, but now the fighting forces took almost all of the young men. Many retired railroad men returned temporarily to fill jobs within a brigade that included a stationmaster, seven assistant stationmasters, 29 gateman, 75 information clerks, 150 redcaps, 15 matrons and maids, and a skilled team of 335 scrubbers, moppers, dusters, polishers, and window cleaners.

The redcaps themselves were like a small army within the Terminal, and they functioned like one too, with a chief, two assistant chiefs, a lieutenant, and sixteen captains. Chief James H. Williams, who joined the Terminal workforce in 1903, was the first African American man employed at Grand Central as a redcap. Supervising close to 300 men, he made sure they all did their jobs well, taking charge of long-distance travelers' luggage and steering them in the right direction. Before any of his men went on to the floor they had to pass Williams's inspection.

One of Chief Williams's men was Ralston Crosbie Young, redcap No. 42, known as "the Red Cap Preacher" of Grand Central because of the prayer meetings he led on track 13. A multiracial group of seven men would meet at the golden clock every Monday, Wednesday, and Friday at noon and accompany Young to an empty railroad car for a twenty-minute prayer service. When once asked if he wanted to trade his job for a more suitable arena for a ministry, Young replied, "I wouldn't change this job now for the biggest pulpit in the city. I mean exactly that . . . Grand Central is a parish, a big one, too, and a mighty good one." Written up in *Reader's Digest* as "The Most Unforgettable Character I've Met," Young received a lot of fan mail, including a letter from an injured soldier returning from World War II. "I had just arrived from overseas," he wrote to Young. "I was trying to quell my hate of people, when you suddenly said, 'Captain, you gotta forgive some of these people. . . . It wasn't so much what you said, although it explained every bit of my feelings. . . . Your words, and the way you said them, were more valuable to me than any other thing. . . ."

The Terminal was flooded with people and soldiers round the clock, so much so that at the height of the war additional emergency ticket offices were added. Women were given unprecedented opportunities during the war, including at Grand Central. In 1942, the New York Central trained fourteen women for service as ticket agents, a position that until then had been held only by

Female ticket agents during World War II welcome customers at one of the Terminal's ticket booth windows.
Collection of New York Central System Historical Society Inc.

men. Bill Hood was assigned to train many of the wartime replacements. He taught the workings of the Terminal and a course in railroad history and folklore. Upon completion of their training, the women ticket agents began on the lower-level windows. If they proved themselves, they were moved to the main ticket windows on the Main Concourse. Hood would always warn the ticket sellers who worked the late-night shift about Grand Central's ghost, a young girl of eighteen or nineteen who frequented the information booth or a ticket window in the early-morning hours asking for directions to her aunt's home on Lexington Avenue in the East forties. Once Hood claimed a trainman, overhearing her conversation, accompanied her home and when they approached the address the girl had given him she disappeared. As the story goes, an elder woman answered the door and after he explained what had happened, she told him that her niece had been killed in a gas explosion when Grand Central was being built and that every few years on the anniversary of her death she returns to the Main Concourse in an attempt to find her way home.

Baggage car operator Nick Schmidt feeds the cats who call the car shop in Grand Central home.
Collection of New York Central System Historical Society Inc.

The railroads were a vital communications point and critical to the country's war effort. They transported hundreds of thousands of Americans in and out of uniform, as well as arms, oil, food, and clothing. Because of this, emergency blackout precautions were taken in case of bombings and the six-story walls of glass windows were painted black.

The Terminal reinforced our national commitment to the war effort and reminded people of what our soldiers and Allied troops were fighting for. Advertisements about the war and the railroad stated: "Today's American railroads are moving the greatest military and civilian traffic in all history. Because out of this war time experience there will come the still finer rail transport of tomorrow. . . . A tomorrow when Grand Central Terminal will echo to the footsteps and laughter of a free and triumphant people, bound once more on swift errands of peace."

In 1941, the Farm Security Administration erected a photo mural 118 feet wide and almost 100 feet high on the east wall of the East Balcony. The 22 photographs created a montage of "What America Has to Defend and How It Will Defend It." Part of a campaign to sell U.S. Defense bonds, the inauguration of this exhibit was broadcast nationally and was attended by 3,000 people, once again placing Grand Central as an identifiable home to the nation. Two years later, a new animated mural for a second war loan drive, measuring seventy-five feet high and thirty feet wide, depicted American flags waving in the breeze with bursting bombs, flames, and clouds of smoke in the background. Beneath this mural was the Service Men's Lounge. Equipped with Ping Pong and pool tables, representatives from the USO, a piano, easy chairs, and lunch counters, the lounge was a meeting room for men of all nations. On any given day, it was not unusual to see a kilted Highlander at the coffee bar learning from an American soldier how to dunk a doughnut.

The East Balcony served as the setting for a heroically sized photo mural urging travelers to buy U.S. Defense bonds.

Rothstein/Library of Congress

During World War II the East Balcony served as a Service Men's Lounge. Note the ornately carved drinking fountains under the arched openings.

Photofest

World War II brought its share of tragedies to Grand Central. Many funeral processions and grieving families passed through the Terminal. The military would arrive through the 43rd Street entrance (where the MetLife Building is today) with coffins that would later be claimed by families and placed on trains en route home. But not all homecomings were tragic. Many a soldier and his girlfriend could be spotted standing at opposite corners of the elliptical vaulted space outside the Oyster Bar, exchanging secrets and sweet nothings in the space known as the "Whispering Gallery." Anyone whispering into one of the four corners would be distinctly heard diagonally across the gallery at the other corner as clearly as if the speaker were standing right next to the person and speaking gently into his or her ear. Another space frequented by soldiers and their families was the Traveler's Aid booth, which handled 13,000 wartime travelers a month. Travelers with lost tickets and broken hearts ended up there, as did mothers who had given all the money in their pockets to their sons on furlough and were now unable to afford the train trip back home. And in 1945 a military reservation booth and general travel information center was opened to handle train reservations for servicemen, supervised by the Army Transportation Corps.

No one was untouched by the war. Pullman cars that had normally brought children home from camp a day or two after Labor Day were needed for troops and wartime services. Even the glamorous star-studded Twentieth Century Limited had to make concessions. On December 7, 1942—the first anniversary of Pearl Harbor—the Century and the Broadway schedule was lengthened to 17 hours in order to make more stops, by direction of the Office of Defense Transportation. Changes were made in some of the bedroom/master cars to meet the minimum sleeping space required by wartime restrictions. Multiple berths that were often taken by single occupants became shared space. Meals were simplified because of food rationing.

Despite all of this, rail travel continued to increase. During the closing years of World War II the New York Central was able to afford the capital improvement to the Terminal that it had wanted to begin some twenty years before, starting with the renovation of the sky ceiling. This renovation was combined with plans to paint the frames of the windows at the ends of the Main Concourse and to clean the imitation Caen stone walls. Given all that this great room meant to Americans, the renovation signaled a time of renewal and hope. Between August and September of 1944, a huge scaffold was suspended to accomplish the work. It was auspiciously completed in 1945. With the end of World War II in 1945, the prewar services of the Twentieth Century Limited were resumed, and people had the joy of seeing the red carpet rolled out at Grand Central once again.

In 1947, over 65 million people—the equivalent of 40 percent of the U.S. population—traveled the rails via Grand Central Terminal. The men in the Philosophers' Gallery and the Service Men's Lounge were now replaced with bench sitters like William Priestly who, at seventy-two, came to the terminal almost every day to sit on a bench and watch the crowds. Retired from a shipping company, he said, "Somehow, ships never meant much to me. From the time I was a kid I wanted to be a railroader but just never got the chance. Now I like to sit here on these benches, just to be close to the trains. For me, it's more fun than going to a movie or a baseball game. It's the most exciting place in New York City, and it's different every day."

The arrival of heavyweight boxing champion Joe Louis was a cause for celebration for the redcaps of Grand Central.
Corbis/Bettmann ©

One of the millions of faces of Grand Central, Frank Sinatra is helped through a teeming crowd of lovesick fans in 1943.
Corbis/Bettmann ©

The Lost and Found also took on a different demeanor in the late 1940s. Strange items were still left on the trains but the car walkers were gone. Instead, suburban commuters often left things on the train in the morning on purpose and claimed them later in the day so that they didn't have to carry them around. There was one particular commuter who became famous in the Lost and Found. A stockbroker from Connecticut, he would leave his sixteen-pound bowling ball

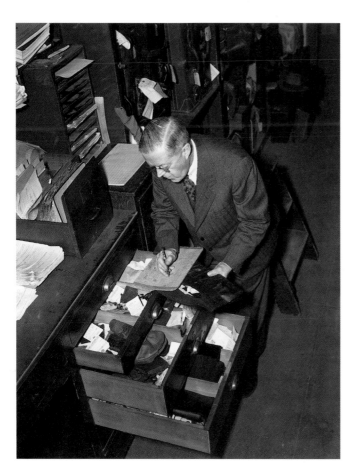

in a specially designed canvas bag every Thursday morning, and at the end of the workday he'd call the Lost and Found and pick up his ball for the game that evening. Finally the brakeman on the local, after carrying the sixteen pounds up the stairs from the tracks each week for six weeks, realized that the stockbroker was using him as a free redcap service. On the seventh Thursday, when the broker appeared to claim his bowling ball, there was a message from the brakeman saying that the next time he found that ball on the local this side of Stamford he was going to drop it off in Cos Cob Creek. The sixteen-pound bowling ball never appeared again.

Even in peacetime Grand Central was home to many unusual events. When a circus train was unloaded at Grand Central Terminal, it was found that two of the elephants were too big to walk through the largest doors in the terminal. After great discussion and some panic, the circus discovered that if the elephants could kneel and crawl out on their stomachs, with the help of an experienced trainer, they could fit through the exit at the taxi ramp. In the early 1950s, thirty-five Los Angeles policemen rode through Grand Central on their motorcycles. The moment their train arrived for an American Legion convention they shot out of a baggage car with a thundering roar and rode straight up the train platform into the station, across the Concourse, through the Waiting Room, out the main door, and down 42nd Street, sirens screaming.

During the Depression years Grand Central Terminal had symbolized safety to the psyches of the economically disinherited. To the returning soldiers of World War II, it was like a great nondenominational cathedral. But whether it was home to travelers, soldiers, poets, or children, Grand Central Terminal remained the gateway to a million lives.

With a thunderous roar, 35 Los Angeles motorcycle cops raced out of their train, through terminal on way to Legion convention

Collier's for March 5, 1954

Elephant boy had to force charge to knees so animal could be squeezed through a taxi ramp

Cartoonist Eric Gurney in *Collier's* magazine captured the humor in many real-life episodes at Grand Central.

Courtesy of Eric Gurney Trust

A familiar scene to many New Yorkers, parents and their children fill the Main Concourse for summer camp departure.

AP/Wide World Photos

When summer camp ends, Grand Central is invaded by 32,000 children, their relatives, pet lizards, snakes, turtles, rabbits, frogs

A minister and a farmer met in concourse to swap false teeth. They lost dentures on the train, took wrong sets at Lost and Found

CHAPTER SIX

GRAND CENTRAL OF THE IMAGINATION

The art of dancing stands at the source of all the arts that express themselves first in the human person. The art of the building, or architecture, is the beginning of all the arts that lie outside the person; and in the end they unite.
—HAVELOCK ELLIS, *THE DANCE OF LIFE*

Grand Central Terminal is great architecture and great art. Many accomplished writers, filmmakers, performers, and artists have embraced its grandeur and mythological quality, beginning with its first incarnation: the Depot, a large space with embellished wrought-iron arches and an ornate glass-and-iron curtain wall. Trains approaching Grand Central, which could number up to 130 daily, were signaled by heavy clouds of steam. In *A Hazard of New Fortunes*, written in 1890, William Dean Howells describes Isabel March's departure for her trip to Boston from the Depot. "The coming and going of the trains marking the station with vivider or fainter plumes of flame-shot steam—formed an incomparable perspective. . . . They paused in the gallery that leads from the elevated station to the waiting rooms in the Central Depot and looked down upon the great night trains lying on the tracks dim under the rain of gaslights that starred without dispersing the vast darkness of the place."

The Grand Central Depot's expansion in 1900 included a new concourse and waiting room. The waiting room walls were made of Breche violet marble and the floors of white Italian marble. After the Depot was razed, the newly electrified Terminal had a plethora of underground tunnels and labyrinths to accommodate miles of new train tracks. In his 1938 classic *You Can't Go Home Again*, Thomas Wolfe reflected on this industrial world when he describes Mr. Jack's fascination with the rumbling trains beneath a newly transformed Park Avenue built over railroad tracks. "The man told him that the great apartment house had been built across two depths of railway tunnels, and that all Mr. Jack had felt was the vibration that came from the passing of a train deep in the bowels of the earth. The man assured him that it was all quite safe, that the very trembling in the walls, in fact, was just another proof of safety. 'Great trains pass

Stephan Koplowitz and dancers perform "Fenestrations" along the glass-enclosed catwalks, using one of Grand Central's most dramatic spaces as the setting for this imaginative dance piece as part of Grand Central Dances in 1987.
Courtesy of MTA/Metro-North Collection, Frank English photographer

under me,' he thought. . . . All of them come looking for the same magic want. Power. Power. Power."

The Terminal descends five stories below street level with a maze of steam pipes, spun cables, and electric generators that created the setting for a modern-day *Les Miserables* in Jennifer Toth's 1993 *The Mole People*. Though it has been debated whether this is a fictionalized account or not, the book focuses on the homeless people who lived in the Dantesque subway tunnels and hidden

spaces beneath Grand Central. Sue MacVeigh's 1939 *Grand Central Murder* describes another protagonist's obsession with the tunnels below this masterpiece. "Stories or rather legends about the steam tunnels tangled my thoughts. . . . I never had believed any of the yarns; they didn't seem possible when you knew terminal employees constantly patrolled the place and worked in it— yet now they plagued me."

Fascination with Hades below 42nd Street extended to filmmakers. In the 1978 *Superman*, arch-

Cary Grant evades the authorities by blending into the crowd at Grand Central in Alfred Hitchcock's *North by Northwest*, 1959.

The Kobal Collection

villain Lex Luthor hides in tunnels beneath Grand Central that were actually created on a separate sound stage recreating this imaginative world below this Beaux Arts wonder. The 1982 thriller *A Stranger Is Watching*, in which a psychopath takes a mother and child prisoner in a secret underground cavern, was shot in the real Terminal. Characters vanished within the labyrinth of Grand Central in many different ways. A person could simply disappear by slipping into the rush hour crowds. Hitchcock used the Main Concourse for this purpose in his 1959 *North by Northwest*. Wearing sunglasses to disguise himself from the police, Cary Grant rushes through the Main Concourse and escapes, undetected, aboard the Twentieth Century Limited for Chicago. Grand Central's ticket windows (and a ticket seller) also play a role in this movie. Grand Central had already appeared in an earlier Hitchcock film. His 1945 *Spellbound* has Gregory Peck trying not to rescind his identity but to recover it. In a desperate attempt to regain his memory, Peck, an amnesiac who has been accused of murder, flees with psychiatrist Ingrid Bergman from a ticket window at Penn Station to one at Grand Central. They escape, boarding a train to Rochester at track 29. This scene captured on film the temporary transformation of Grand

Central during wartime and highlights both of New York's great train stations.

Grand Central may have seen the likes of Gregory Peck, Cary Grant, and Ingrid Bergman, but it is the character Holden Caulfield in J. D. Salinger's 1945 *Catcher in the Rye* that remains one of the most memorable and universal to

Ingrid Bergman and Gregory Peck board a train from Grand Central in Alfred Hitchcock's 1945 *Spellbound.*
The Kobal Collection

have passed through the Terminal's doors. "I walked over to Lexington, and took the subway down to Grand Central. My bags were there and all and I figured I'd sleep in that crazy waiting room where all the benches are. So that's what I did. It wasn't too bad for a while because there weren't many people around and I could stick my feet up. But I don't feel much like discussing it. It wasn't too nice. Don't ever try it. I mean it. It'll depress you." When Salinger wrote Holden Caulfield's words, just after the end of World War II, he was probably unaware of how prophetic they were to be about Grand Central's future. Once again, fact and fiction were bound into the very fabric of the architecture.

Forty years later, in the same waiting room on one of the now worn and weathered wooden benches, Lee Stringer in *Grand Central Winter, Stories from the Street* writes about being homeless and sleeping in the Terminal. By this time the Waiting Room was showing signs of age and neglect. The chandeliers no longer glittered, the Tennessee pink marble floors were worn, and the Caen stone sheathing was stained with pollution. "It hadn't been too long before that we could have camped out on the benches of Grand Central's main waiting room at night. . . . I never elected to sleep in the waiting room myself. The place was the scene of a continuous, boisterous, often drunken bacchanal. And while that could be a lot of fun during the day, it was not conducive to more restful pursuits."

Superman (Christopher Reeve) visits arch-villain Lex Luthor (Gene Hackman) at his palace located in the depths of Grand Central Terminal (actually, a studio set) in *Superman,* **1978.**
The Kobal Collection

Ninety feet above the Main Concourse floor, a camera crew films Kelly McGillis. Her character is crawling along the cornice of the Main Concourse trying to escape from Mandy Patinkin in the 1988 remake of *The House on Carroll Street*.

Courtesy of MTA/Metro-North Collection, Frank English photographer

There are other architectural details within Grand Central's lofty 80,000 square foot Main Concourse that have inspired larger-than-life moments for writers and filmmakers. "Meet me at the clock" is an expression identified with Grand Central. Many romances have begun and ended at the clock, so it is befitting that the "golden clock" in *The Fisher King* is the centerpiece for Robin Williams's fantasy of dancing with his dream girl during the evening rush hour. As he follows her across the crowded Main Concourse their meeting transforms the hectic rush hour into a sublime dance scene where everyone is waltzing around the brass clock. The constellation ceiling with its 2,500 stars and astrological signs on a cerulean blue background remains one of Grand Central's most recognizable and iconographic images. As seen through the eyes of Peter Lake in Mark Helprin's *Winter's Tale*, "It was as if the building itself had been skillfully constructed to mirror life on earth and its ultimate consequences, and to reflect the way in which men went about their business mostly without looking up, unaware that they were gliding about on the bottom of a vast sea. From the shadows of the gallery above Vanderbilt Avenue, Peter Lake looked above him and saw the sky and constellations majestically portrayed against the huge barreled vault that floated overhead. It was one of the few places in the world where the darkness and the light floated like clouds and clashed under a ceiling."

The 1988 remake of *The House on Carroll Street* gives us a different perspective of the constellation ceiling—a view behind the scenes, as it were. Kelly McGillis, the heroine, is being chased by Mandy Patinkin, the villain, along the glass bridge behind the middle arched windows on the east side of the Main Concourse. Climbing out of one of the windows she walks onto the building's southeast cornice. There she finds a door that takes her into the attic of the ceiling. (Although the door does not really exist, the attic does.) Once in the attic, she climbs a rope ladder and kicks her pursuer backwards through the ceiling to his death 125 feet below on the marble floor. Before falling through the plaster board he rips through the black netting that workers in the Terminal actually use to walk on in order to service light bulbs. In filming the fall, a stunt man was raised by a cable through a hole in the ceiling that had been made in the 1960s in order to display a rocket.

Dancers, singers, and solo performance artists, inspired by Grand Central's architecture, have created works specifically designed for performance within the building. Grand Central Dances on October 9–10, 1987, organized by Dancing in the Streets, was one such event. Performed by different dance companies and solo artists including Lucinda Childs, Philippe Petit, and Michael Moschen, it featured Merce Cunningham's troupe opening the evening with a work called "Events" in the Main Concourse, accompanied by a laser-light show by Richard Sandhaus. This was followed by an hour-long work called "Terminal Triptych" in the Incoming Train Room by the twenty-six-member ensemble of Paul Thompson and Troop Three. This site-specific piece was inspired by the room's antique fixtures and its nickname, the "kissing room." Stephan Koplowitz, with a troupe of thirty-six, danced on the glass-encased catwalks in "Fenestrations," a thirteen-minute work about home. Anne Kisselgoff wrote in her review, "Close quarters helped the communal feeling of life and art converging into a genuine, if manufactured, urban rite."

In 1989 the Terminal was host to the Rolling Stones's press conference announcing their Steel Wheels tour; Carly Simon sang live in Grand Central for her 1995 concert for Lifetime Television; and when Madonna, in her 1998 video *Ray of Light*, needed a location that typified the rush of the day, she used Grand Central.

In the climactic chase scene in *The House on Carroll Street,* a stuntman falls from the sky ceiling. A cable that was attached to his body and ran through a small hole in the ceiling to a steel rafter in the attic space broke his fall before he hit the marble floor.

Courtesy of MTA/Metro-North Collection, Frank English photographer

Part of the quality that makes Grand Central such an inviting canvas for artists is the universal identification with this space. And no single work has done more to solidify this image than the half-hour radio drama *Grand Central Station*. For over a decade in the 1940s and 1950s, it broadcast to the homes of millions of people who could experience a ride on the rails into Grand Central without ever having to leave their living rooms. Heard every Saturday morning on CBS, it began with an organ in the background and the sound of train wheels clicking. Its introduction is legendary: "As the bullet seeks its target, shining rails in every part of our great country are aimed at Grrrrand Centrrrral Staaaation, part of the nation's greatest city. Drawn by the magnetic force of the fantastic metropolis, day and night great trains rush toward the Hudson River, sweep down its eastern bank for 140 miles, flash briefly past the long row of tenement

To announce their Steel Wheels tour of 1989, Mick Jagger and the Rolling Stones came to Grand Central's *emotional rescue*.

Courtesy of MTA/Metro-North Collection, Frank English photographer

houses to 125th Street, dive with a roar into the two-and-one-half-mile tunnel beneath the swank and glitter of Park Avenue and then—Grrrrand Centrrrral Staaaation—crossroad of a million private lives, gigantic stage on which are played a thousand dramas, daily."

Himan Brown, the producer and creator of the now-legendary radio drama, said that for the opening sequence he wanted a train with a whistle and a roar. "An electric train doesn't make the chugging sound a steam train does. I couldn't create what I imagined with electric. I visualized the Santa Fe roaring under Park Avenue and that was the sound that people heard every week. Since 'Grand Central Station' was so successful I tried to sell 'International Airport.' I figured it worked with a train, why not an airport, but without Grand Central as the focus it wasn't the same." Actually, the title of the show and what many writers and filmmakers make reference to as Grand Central Station is a misnomer. Its proper name is Grand Central Terminal.

The radio program had many different writers. One of them, Elaine McMahon-Bissell, commented on how her personal relationship with Grand Central influenced her writing. "This is where I came and stood to watch the swarming masses of people on a bitter cold Sunday afternoon, one long ago December, when planes dropped bombs on a faraway place called Pearl Harbor. Much of my life has seeped into those stones, my laughter has echoed there. But even more. It was my palace of make-believe. My heroes and heroines have filed along its train platforms, begun a life of desperate crime at one of its news-stands, restaurants, or gift shops. . . . This is the stuff that dreams were made of, a hundred settings, backgrounds, sound effects, and characters for the poor man's Clifford Odets and Sidney Kingsley, the Iowa farm wife's Philip Barry and Sir James Barry, the Tennessee hill woman's George Bernard Shaw and Irwin Shaw."

In the 1950s, as television began to take over from radio, CBS established a television studio on one of the upper floors above the Waiting Room and start-ed broadcasting programs from Grand Central. Unexpectedly, television viewers began to experi-ence an annoying prob-lem with their reception: images would frequently vibrate on their TV screens. The problem was caused by the trains coming and going from the terminal. Every time a train entered or left,

Located above the Waiting Room, the CBS Studio recorded and broad-cast many programs during the 1940s and 1950s, including the tele-vision show *Studio One* and the radio show *Grand Central Station.* Being televised here is the *CBS Amateur Boxing Night.*
CBS Photo Archive

the building would vibrate; every vibration in the studios above the Waiting Room caused a vibration on individual television screens. (In later years the studios were converted to tennis courts. Located on the third floor, these tennis courts have existed for over twenty years).

The CBS studios were the inadvertent catalyst to a celebrated moment in architectural history when Andy Rooney, then a writer for one of CBS's morning programs, gave Frank Lloyd Wright a seemingly impromptu tour of Grand Central Terminal. Rooney, in Edgar Tafel's book *About Wright*, talks of walking with Wright through Grand Central on their way to the CBS studio, then on the third floor. Wright had been invited to New York for an interview at CBS, and Rooney picked Wright up at the Park Plaza Hotel and delivered him to CBS. "Wright grumbled about everything during the drive from the Plaza to the Vanderbilt Avenue side of Grand Central. He detested New York. I agreed with him about some things, but I love New York and especially Grand Central. There was access by elevator from the west side to our studio but I decided to force a tour on him. . . . I recall clearly that he stopped and looked back across the grand room before we got on the elevator. The sun's rays were slanting down toward the information booth from the windows above where the Kodak picture is now. 'It is a grand building, isn't it?' he said, almost apologetically, and I

The Merce Cunningham Dance Company performs in the Main Concourse.

Courtesy of Dancing in the Streets, Jonathan Atkin photographer

accepted this as a retraction for all the terrible things he'd been saying about everything else. We went to the third floor on the elevator and started across the catwalk. It's one of the great sights in New York for me. Thousands of purposeful people going their own directions and with doors and stairs and levels enough for all of them in Grand Central. Midway across, Wright stopped and neither of us said anything. He must have stood there for more than five minutes, and I didn't speak because I knew nothing I had to say could match what he was thinking. I finally had to tell him we were due very shortly in the studio and he reluctantly finished his crossing of the catwalk. The whole incident gave me a great feeling because I thought I'd had some effect on Frank Lloyd Wright's opinion of my city and I know he could never think completely negatively about it again after his visit to Grand Central. . . ."

Artists and creative thinkers have taken Grand Central into their hearts and individual imagination in unique ways. Dr. Cornel West spoke about Grand Central's transformative powers and magical qualities after a literary PEN (poets, playwrights, essayists, editors, novelists) event. "My fondest memory of the old Grand Central Station is dancing the night away with my wife Elleni at the 1993 spring banquet of the writers' group PEN. When I first arrived at the train station I could not believe my eyes—a genuine architectural transubstantiation had occurred. Instead of a celestial public space for personal transit, I beheld an enchanted place for public feasting. This august group of poets, novelists, and critics wined and dined until we speakers had our say. Then appeared—to our pleasant surprise—a smooth, sophisticated, yet funky band that invited all of us to the dance floor. I think it was my good friend and brother Russell Banks and his wife Chas—or was it Mary Gordon and companion or Rita Dove and husband—who broke the ice. Soon all of us were having a grand time—dancing with, between, and across each other—to the songs of Motown groups, James Brown, and George Clinton played by the hip band. As the night drew to a close, Elleni and I were the last couple on the floor—caught up in the magic of the old Grand Central Station with so many master wordsmiths grooving to music that transcends language."

The restored Waiting Room where Cornel West and fellow writers danced the night away, and the Main Concourse, which rendered Frank Lloyd Wright speechless, are, in the words of the architect of the current restoration, "a place where the surface of the marble is just right, not too slippery. Where your feet glide over the floor with just the right traction and the joints are so tight that there's never any discrepancy between two pieces of marble. You put all these characteristics together and you have a great floor and an inspiring presence. It makes you feel like dancing. It makes you feel like Fred Astaire." When art and architecture converge, it reminds us that architects use design as a form of language in much the same way that writers use words.

Painters have been inspired by Grand Central for decades. In John Sloan's *Grand Central Station* (1924), he portrays a moment in the bustling activity of train travel at that time.
Collection of the Montgomery Museum of Fine Arts, Montgomery Alabama, The Blount Collection

EASTMAN
Kodak
COMPANY

Whatever happens — take your camera

**KODAK**
EXHIBIT CENTER

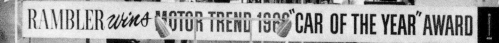
RAMBLER *wins* MOTOR TREND 1963 "CAR OF THE YEAR" AWARD

CHAPTER SEVEN

THE DECLINE OF
GRAND CENTRAL

*No doubt the progressive cannibalization that has been going on in the great con-
course ever since the . . . room was saved in 1954, filling its once magnificent space
with signs, turntables, land-boom selling booths, oversized clocks, and other gim-
micks to turn a quick buck, is all meant to offset declining "railroad" revenues
because the owners are railroads.*

—DOUGLAS HASKELL, *PROGRESSIVE ARCHITECTURE*, OCTOBER 1960

After World War II ended, the glory days of train travel began to decline. Grand
Central no longer had 63 million people passing through its doors as it did in
1946. After a record level of 252,251 daily passengers passed through the Terminal
on July 3, 1947, Grand Central's decline began. By the early 1950s, as urban
growth became suburban and decentralized, the railroad was claiming that it
cost $24 million more to maintain Grand Central than it took in as income.

Americans were displaying their strong national preference for indepen-
dence and the freedom to choose to live and work outside the perceived constraints of more crowded and older cities. The birth of suburban America was
not a spontaneous occurrence, but the result of deliberate federal government
policies that changed the face of urban America. G.I. loans and mortgages fueled
the postwar suburban housing boom. Low-density suburbs rapidly took shape
on the outskirts of older cities that, because of their dense compact form, had
been well served by the railroads. The railroads were unable to provide the same
regular, affordable, and convenient service to these far-flung and sprawling bed-
room communities without massive infusions of new capital, something the railroad companies did not possess and the government was not about to provide.
Government had chosen instead to support the newer forms of transportation:
automobiles, trucks, and airplanes.

In the 1950s the federal government started crisscrossing the country with
a new, vast, interstate highway system, funded initially on the premise that it
was a necessary component of national defense. The aircraft industry, using the
research and production resources it had developed during the war, had the

A new 1960s Rambler on display in
the Main Concourse steals the spot-
light. Ironically, this advertisement
provided quick revenue for the
declining railroad, which was being
replaced by automobiles.
Photograph by Peter Fink

capacity for the first time to build a new, exciting product to supply to a rapidly growing airlines business: the fast and efficient jetliner.

Americans were becoming less dependent upon intercity train travel and nothing illustrated this more dramatically than the decline of the great steel fleets of the Limiteds. First they suffered the indignity of pulling day coaches as part of their payload, then their service was reduced until, unable to compete with the airlines, they disappeared completely. Much of the Century's fleet surfaced south of the border in the late 1960s as part of the Mexican National Railroad.

As revenues from passenger and freight traffic declined, the railroad's owners began to compensate by exploiting their real estate assets. Grand Central's troubles began to accelerate. With declining traffic, it wasn't the Terminal that would stimulate redevelopment, but rather exploitation by property speculators. In the late 1940s the stable, mid-rise, fashionable residential community that had existed for over a quarter of a century along Park Avenue and above Grand Central's tracks between 46th and 59th streets fell into the hands of real estate speculators intent on turning the area into a fashionable high-rise office district.

A 1949 aerial view of Levittown on Long Island shows the explosion of suburban sprawl, fueled by the automobile and the highway.

Corbis/Bettmann ©

Between 1952 and 1979, more than fifteen hotels, apartment buildings, and other structures that had been conceived and erected as part of Terminal City, with a cohesiveness of architectural style, materials, and mass, were demolished to make room for larger and mostly architecturally banal office buildings. The twelve-story Montana Apartments became the forty-story Seagram Building; the twelve-story Marguery at 270 Park gave way to the fifty-two-story Union Carbide headquarters; and at 277 Park another twelve-story apartment building was replaced by the fifty-story Chemical Bank building. Despite public opposition, all this was accomplished with the participation of the railroad company, who owned the tracks and the platforms above which the new construction was taking place.

By the 1950s, the New York Central was battered by steep declines in its railroad business. Without government assistance the railroad was held captive by stock speculators who were more interested in turning quick profits from the real estate boom than in nurturing back to health the business of transporting people and goods. The Terminal itself became a massive billboard and its dignified interior was systematically obliterated by commercial messages. In 1950, the Kodak Corporation installed a giant 18 foot by 65 foot screen on the East Balcony overlooking the Main Concourse—probably the most prominent location in the entire Terminal—beaming down on a captive audience huge images that dwarfed the Concourse. A 30-foot diameter clock advertising *Newsweek*

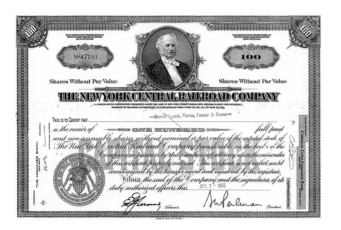

On a stock certificate dated 1955, Cornelius Vanderbilt watches his railroad empire crumble through stock manipulation.

Courtesy of MTA/Metro-North Collection

was suspended above the ramp linking the Waiting Room and the Main Concourse just a few short steps from the jewel-like clock atop the information booth. Merrill Lynch erected an informational booth with a large ticker-tape display in the middle of the public circulation space of the Main Concourse. And the Chrysler Corporation rented space from which they proudly displayed their latest automobiles.

Along with this was the railroad management's attempt to successfully emulate the real estate speculation of Park Avenue. In 1954, after many years of persistence, a stock manipulator from Texas named Robert R. Young finally succeeded in gaining a controlling interest of the New York Central. Having little success in merging the Central with other railroads, he began to look to the railroad's real estate as the next source of revenue. The first real estate plan sponsored by the New York Central was a proposal in 1954 by Webb & Knapp, a nationally prominent real estate developer, for a dramatic 108-story tower in the shape of a hyperboloid to replace the Terminal. The architect was a youthful I. M. Pei who, as Marcel Breuer would later, demonstrated that his first priority was to design a modern icon rather than retain the historic Terminal.

Robert Young and the New York Central Railroad shared the interest of Grand Central Terminal with the New York, New Haven and Hartford Railroad, led by president Patrick McGinnis. Later in 1954, a few months after the I. M. Pei plan was proposed by Young, Patrick McGinnis with the consultation of developer Erwin Wolfson proposed a $4 million, fifty-five story office tower and railroad complex over Park Avenue calling for the demolition of Grand Central. The architects for the plan were Fellheimer and Wagner, the successor firm of Reed & Stem.

From 1954 to 1958, the plans proposed by the New York Central Railroad and the New York, New Haven and Hartford remained unbuilt as the railroads labored to sustain their operations with no plan to work together on real estate development. In order for a building project of this scale to begin, the two corporate giants had to join forces; they did so in 1958 with an agreement made by Young and McGinnis to use Erwin Wolfson as their developer in the creation of Grand Central City.

Wolfson proposed a 3 million square foot, fifty-story office tower to be built on the site of the six-story Grand Central Terminal office and baggage facility in between the Terminal and the New York Central Building (now the

"Great Scott! Now what's happened?"

The demise of railroad travel had commuters comforting conductors.

Drawing by Peter Arno; © 1963 The New Yorker Magazine, Inc.

Helmsley Building). In July 1958, architects Walter Gropius and Pietro Belluschi were hired to team up with Emery Roth & Sons, forming a prominent design team for the Grand Central City project. In 1959, the tower was seen as an architectural and engineering feat. By 1963, a 2.4 million square foot, fifty-nine-story, octagonal tower was complete, named the Pan Am Building (now the MetLife Building), since Pan Am was the majority tenant.

The New York Central achieved little or no economic relief from these excessively commercial exploitations of the Terminal, and the overall effect on its appearance and day-to-day condition was abysmal. More time and investment went into grandiose development planning than conserving the existing masterpiece and running the railroad efficiently. With passenger and freight traffic continuing to decline at a rapid rate, it was clear that if it was going to survive, the Central had no choice but to attempt to finalize a merger with its deadly rival, Pennsylvania Railroad. In 1958, right in the middle of intense negotiations between Robert Young and Pennsylvania Railroad's president James Symes, Young committed suicide. By 1961, an agreement was signed between the two railroads, but due to government regulations the actual merger was not finalized until 1968, creating the Penn Central Corporation.

From the first year of the new Penn Central Corporation the merger was a failure. The combination of the two railroads' management teams was unable to develop a cohesive operation. With the Pennsylvania Railroad's senior management remaining in Philadelphia and New York Central's being in New York City, confusion was an everyday event. Sometimes entire freight trains would be "lost," only to turn up hundreds of miles away from their intended destinations. Not surprisingly, the railroad lost a lot of business to the trucking industry through such inefficiency.

By 1970, Penn Central had lost over $100 million in the year's first quarter. The country was in a recession, the stock market plunged, and the government refused to bail out the railroad. With rolling stock and locomotives needing urgent repairs, many miles of track virtually unusable, stations falling apart, signalization systems burning out, and steel bridges and structures covered with rust, there was no choice but to file for bankruptcy.

Penn Central persisted in its attempts to regain its economic health through the exploitation of its valuable real estate. In 1968 it joined forces with British developer Morris Saady in a proposal to build a skyscraper by Marcel

Opposite: As railroad revenues continued to decline through the 1950s and 1960s, commercial booths and advertising messages continued to fill the Terminal.
© Beyer Blinder Belle Architects & Planners

The plaster entablature and Caen stone walls of the Main Concourse show the decades of dirt and decay prior to the restoration.
© James Rudnick Photography

Thousands of people fill the Main Concourse on May 24, 1962, riveted by the live coverage of the historic launch of the Atlas Rocket carrying astronaut M. Scott Carpenter.

Corbis/Bettmann ©

Breuer directly above the Terminal. The first version was to be sited on top of the Main Concourse; the second version above the Waiting Room and the south-facing facade. Despite the continued rejection of this proposal by the New York City Landmarks Commission, Breuer's response reflected the boundless confidence and arrogance of the era: "The Landmarks Preservation Commission is preventing the usefulness and natural growth of the city. Sooner or later, there is absolutely no doubt a skyscraper will be built above the Terminal." It was symptomatic of the times that historical perspective was so negligible and avarice so unlimited. What followed was years of legal battles in the state's courts and eventually in the U.S. Supreme Court.

As Grand Central was fighting for its life, the country was in a time of great change and conflict. The year 1963 brought a mass march to Washington, at which time Martin Luther King, Jr., delivered an impassioned and brilliant speech. Subsequently, President Lyndon Johnson succeeded in passing a sweeping civil rights act in 1964 that prohibited discrimination in public facilities and in employment. That same year brought rioting in America's major cities in protest against the casual violence of the police toward the black community. "Long, hot summers" became part of urban life. Increased racial tensions were one element of the country's social and political climate. The continuing war in Vietnam reached its height between 1966 and 1969; in 1968 domestic opposition to the war reached a new level; 1967, the summer of love and the popularization of the hippie movement brought vast numbers of predominately white youth into violent contact with the law. It was within this climate that another movement of grass-roots protest was born: the historic preservation movement. The fight to save Grand Central would become one of its earliest causes, turning a fledgling group into a national force that would shape the future of our cities by fighting to preserve the best of our past.

In the spring of 1968, groups as diverse as historic preservationists and youthful activists for social change found Grand Central to be a strong symbol of their causes. One evening in March 1968, a Yip-In was held to promote the Yippies' Festival of Life. "Come to Grand Central at Midnight," the flyers read. When the organizers were asked what the political or tactical reason was for choosing Grand Central, the response was simple: "It's Central, man." An estimated 6,000 people filled the Main Concourse with chants like "Long, Hot Summer" and "Burn, Baby, Burn." Just before 1:00 A.M. some of the crowd began climbing on the roof of the information booth, striking a "workers arise" fist-in-the-air pose. Two cherry bombs exploded and someone grabbed the hands off the information clock. "I was standing on the balcony looking down," remembers Clark Whelton, a former reporter for the *Village Voice*. "When I looked down, I saw this guy holding the hands from the clock and I saw a police officer take a nightstick and knock it on the marble balustrade. You could hear that sound reverberate through the crowd. Suddenly a flying wedge of cops charged into the Concourse. The crowd and the cops went wild. Most of the people being arrested were automatically beaten with nightsticks."

Long after the Yippies were gone the historic preservationists continued their fight to save a building that was rapidly mirroring the demise of its owners

New York police break up the Festival of Life gathering of the Youth International Party ("Yippies") in the Main Concourse in the spring of 1968.

and the surrounding social climate. A terminal that had not closed its doors for over sixty years was now locked up each night for several hours. The growing population of the homeless, with increasingly fewer options, looked at Grand Central as home. "One day I saw a girl and a fella run in through the entrance near the Waiting Room as if they had entered the front door of their own home," recounted Robert L. Smith, the current assistant stationmaster. "There was something so private about this public display. They were arguing and she kept yelling, 'get out of my house, this is my house, why don't you go over to Penn Station and live.'"

Keeping the bathrooms clean and safe was growing impossible as more and more homeless New Yorkers used the space to bathe and launder their clothing. The railroad leased the restrooms to a private concession hoping they could do a better maintenance job. "The walls and ceilings of grand public rooms are stained and dingy, a jumble of telephone booths, vending machines, baggage lockers and newspaper kiosks have robbed the building of its dignity," wrote a reporter in 1975. Crime became a problem. The building was divided into turf claimed by different drug dealers. Grand Central got the reputation among New Yorkers of being unsafe and unsavory. It became a place to avoid. Commuters were scared to take trains there at night. Parents warned their

With long-distance train travel rapidly retreating from Grand Central, the stately Waiting Room once used by passengers heading to Boston, Buffalo, or Chicago became a temporary home for many disenfranchised New Yorkers in the 1970s and 1980s as the railroad permitted it to fall further into neglect.

Courtesy of MTA/Metro-North Collection, Frank English photographer

children not to use the dangerous bathrooms. The profound neglect and decay of Grand Central Terminal was simply one more casualty in the decline of the nation's urban cities.

In 1978, after ten years of court cases and appeals, the Supreme Court upheld the landmark status of the building and found for the City of New York. More was gained than the Terminal itself. The court's ruling set a standard that cities should protect their heritage. We as a city and a country were now being challenged to look at our built environment with fairness, vision, and integrity.

"What the hell do you mean you don't sell tickets to Larchmont?"

CHAPTER EIGHT

THE RESTORATION
CAST ASSEMBLES

Don't put your money into railway stations.
—JOHN RUSKIN, *THE STONES OF VENICE*

The preservation victory in the Supreme Court was just the beginning of the hard work ahead for Grand Central. For the private citizens who had fought so hard to save the Terminal it was a period of disillusion. Although the building was no longer threatened by demolition and was in the hands of an accountable public agency, where were the funds to bring back its glory?

In 1978 New York State's Metropolitan Transportation Authority (the MTA) took over the day-to-day management of Grand Central from Penn Central. Five years later, it established the Metro-North Commuter Railroad to run the three regional lines that operated out of the Terminal. When Metro-North began its operations one minute after midnight on January 1, 1983, the friends of Grand Central thought they had finally found effective guardians for the building. But in an economic climate so bleak that entire cities, including New York, were on the brink of bankruptcy, the Terminal's future, though no longer threatened by the wrecking ball, remained dismal.

Metro-North's first president, Peter E. Stangl, had a steep mountain to climb. He knew that a restored and modernized Grand Central would be a powerful symbol of his plans to overhaul the country's second largest regional railroad. However, it would not be easy to obtain the funding needed for the railroad's modernization of its rolling stock, tracks, signals, and safety systems as well as the funds needed to reverse the Terminal's deteriorating condition. If any of this was to be accomplished successfully, he and his associates would have to deal with Grand Central's stewardship in a comprehensive and long-range manner.

Stangl, himself a daily commuter on Metro-North, set out to instill in his employees a sense of caring for the fabric of the Terminal that would parallel their more usual railroad engineering duties. Arriving in the Terminal each morning, he might notice a burned-out light over the prominently located information

A detail of an early rendering (1988) by Piyawat Pattanapuckdee of Beyer Blinder Belle illustrates how to animate the Terminal as a grand and versatile public space.

© Beyer Blinder Belle Architects & Planners

booth; rather than head for his office to issue a memo, he was just as likely to seek out one of the stationmaster's maintenance crew members and point it out. He regularly rode on all the lines, meeting and quickly learning the names of the railroad's personnel. The fact that he didn't rule from a glass tower but in a more personable manner made his impact more effective in a world where collaboration and comradeship had always been the tradition.

Stangl had come to his appointment as Metro-North's president by a somewhat unconventional route. He had worked in the public sector since the idealistic days of Mayor John Lindsay's administration. When burnout loomed, he left public service and supported himself by playing pool professionally in the pool halls of Atlantic City and up and down the East Coast. These experiences shaped his leadership style. He brought to the railroad an approach that, while respecting railroad traditions, was intent on achieving change in a building that he saw as both a railroad asset and powerful, inspiring architecture.

Under Stangl's leadership, Metro-North's first five-year capital program, for 1982–86, allocated $12 million for a careful mix of projects. $4.5 million went for roof repair; while Lee Harris Pomeroy was repairing the Terminal's roof, his fellow architect Giorgio Cavaglieri was restoring the Bottocino marble and ornamental plasterwork of the Incoming Waiting Room, which in 1980 had become one of the Terminal's significant interior spaces to be designated as a landmark space. $4 million of the budget was utilized to develop plans to increase ridership. When executed, the North End Access passages under the sidewalks of Park Avenue would lead travelers as far north as 48th Street and would reduce the travel time of almost half of Metro-North's daily northbound riders by as much as ten to fifteen minutes per trip and, it was hoped, increase ridership by almost one million people a year.

In 1993, Jacqueline Kennedy Onassis presented an award to Peter E. Stangl, president of Metro-North Railroad. In the background are Hugh Hardy, Brendan Gill, and Philip Johnson, who all played major roles in saving Grand Central.
Courtesy of MTA/Metro-North Collection, Frank English photographer

Though the rain no longer poured through the terminal roof, decades of neglect were still visible throughout the stained and damaged interior. Metro-North continued to make small strides and improvements with its limited funds, but relamping historic chandeliers and erasing layers of commercial messages from the limestone walls were not considered critical to the railroad's daily function. The citizens who had fought to save the building from extinction had other ideas. They were now beginning to dream about a future for Grand Central into the twenty-first century. In 1988, to celebrate the Terminal's seventy-fifth birthday and to help focus public attention on this issue, a series of exciting events took place. Architect Hugh Hardy and his colleagues at the Municipal Art Society mounted an exhibit on the Terminal to show the public something

As part of the two-day festival, Grand Central Dances, aerialist Philippe Petit's high-wire act draws the crowd's attention to the derelict state of the sky ceiling.

Courtesy of Dancing in the Streets, Jonathan Atkin photographer

of its remarkable history; using historical photographs the exhibit revealed some of the glories that had long been covered up, altered, or removed. Economist Katherine Welch Howe developed marketing strategies to rejuvenate its retail and cultural facilities. Public events such as a three-day dance festival and art exhibits brought Grand Central into the vision of more and more New Yorkers.

All this attention to Grand Central brought an overwhelming public response that, together with the Municipal Art Society's and architectural community's continued commitment, persuaded Metro-North that the best way to move forward would be to commission a restoration master plan. The purpose of the master plan would be to describe a vision for the building's future—a road map describing the problems, how to solve them, what the costs would be, how to use funding as it became available, and what potential strategies could be explored for securing the Terminal's future. Stangl believed that the task, though challenging, was not insurmountable and that without a master plan there would be no long-term, broad-based public support on which to move ahead and obtain the funds necessary to restore the Terminal.

A public selection process to choose a design team was initiated in the fall of 1988. Many architectural firms responded and eight finalists, all of whom had enormous stature in the architectural community, were chosen for this highly sought after commission. The Beyer Blinder Belle consortium, of which we, the authors, were original members, was selected to create the master plan. Carefully assembled to represent all of the restoration, design, and engineering skills needed, the consortium consisted of fourteen professional firms. Harry

Weese Associates, architects for Union Station, Washington, D.C.; STV/SSVK, engineers for many large-scale and high-profile transportation projects; Fisher, Marantz, Renfro, Stone, lighting designers for Ellis Island; and Vignelli Associates, graphic and signage designers for the New York City Transit system, were the key players on the Beyer Blinder Belle team. Knowing that the competition for the commission would be intense, the team spent many hours refining every detail of their presentation, rehearsing with a director for their big performance. We even had sound effects, with historic audiotapes of train sounds playing discreetly in the background as the interviewing committee assembled.

Beyer Blinder Belle's work on the restoration of Ellis Island, another nationally important historic public space, was a critical factor in the decision. When our team was informed that the selection committee wanted to tour Ellis Island with the architects present, we were in Salt Lake City restoring the Cathedral of the Madeleine. The only way to get back to New York in time for the walk-through the following morning was to head even farther west and catch the red-eye from Las Vegas. Sitting amid the pinball machines and one-armed bandits at the Las Vegas Airport seemed incongruous. Here we were frantic to board an airplane in Las Vegas to win a commission to restore a railroad station in New York.

The champagne celebration on the afternoon of the news of our success was followed the next morning with the first planning and strategy session. Metro-North (as the client) and the restoration team knew that in order to capture public support something needed to be visible to the Terminal's everyday users as soon as possible. We needed something that would have a big impact but not cost big construction dollars. Preparing and implementing the master

The successful restoration of Ellis Island's main building was a major factor in MTA/Metro-North's selection of their architect.
© Sherman Morss, Jr., Finegold Alexander & Associates

plan would be very time-consuming with no immediately visible signs of change until the process was well under way.

We concluded that with one preemptive strike, it would be relatively simple and inexpensive to show the public something of the real Grand Central by dismantling the Kodak sign. The challenge from Stangl's point of view was that Kodak paid about $450,000 to Metro-North Railroad for the privilege of beaming down the larger-than-life images of sailboats and family gatherings. So when the sign's dismantling was discussed as a strategy Stangl knew this would be more than a symbolic gesture. Relinquishing such large advertising dollars, the railroad would signal a real commitment to the citizens who had fought so hard to save the building. Stangl gave his consent and the dismantling began.

Working mostly at night behind shielding drapes through the late winter and early spring of 1990, workers removed the Kodak images and screen piece by piece. Then the exposed marble and simulated limestone walls of the balcony were given a preliminary cleaning before their public reentrance. The morning after the dismantling was finished and the protective curtain was taken down, the architects stood quietly watching the first commuters stream into the Main Concourse from the train platforms. As the sunshine burst through three windows that had not been seen since 1950, it was as if life were being breathed back into the building. Many commuters stopped in their tracks, speechless and amazed at the change that had so instantly brought back the majesty of the space.

The response from the public was overwhelmingly positive and support for the restoration began to grow. The simple yet dramatic change to the Concourse had shown the public just a sample of the wonders that were to come. This event not only affected the commuters, it brought attention from the press, who began to take Metro-North's plans seriously. Building on this favorable reaction, the MTA announced the ambitious $425 million master plan for the complete restoration of the building and their commitment to move the plan forward with funding from their next capital program, scheduled for 1992–96.

Important support for the master plan came from Jacqueline Kennedy Onassis who, at Peter Stangl's and Kent Barwick's invitation, came to hear the Beyer Blinder Belle team make a presentation of their plans. It was a memorable occasion. After a somewhat lengthy talk, the restoration architect thought that the former First Lady and Grand Central's champion had had her fill of the subject and was eager to leave. As she rose from her seat, he thought she was heading for the door. To his surprise she proceeded to engage him in an animated conversation about many of the details of the plan. This brief but intense conversation was an inspiration to the team that was drawn upon many times as future difficulties and frustrations sapped our spirits. Once again, her presence and support made a difference.

On the first Sunday in June, a wonderful early-summer day, the *New York Times's* architectural critic Paul Goldberger began his review of the master

The dismantling of the Kodak sign liberated the East Balcony of the Main Concourse after four decades of blocked sunlight.

above right: © James Rudnick Photography

others: © Beyer Blinder Belle Architects & Planners, James W. Rhodes photographer

The cleaned patch of sky ceiling revealed the brilliant color that lay beneath years of dirt and grime. Some commuters thought the patch was spotlighted. In reality, the cleaned ceiling had no more lighting than the surrounding unrestored ceiling.
© Ross Muir Photographer

The experimental test-cleaning of the sky ceiling occurred on a platform suspended from the southeast corner of the Main Concourse behind a shroud of black netting.
© Beyer Blinder Belle Architects & Planners, James W. Rhodes photographer

plan with the headlines: "Grand Central Basks in a Burst of Morning Light; who would ever have thought you would see the United Nations Secretariat Building from within Grand Central Terminal?" Seeing how successful this first step had been, the restoration team found another opportunity to lift up the eyes of the Grand Central commuter. At the Cathedral of the Madeleine, Beyer Blinder Belle had test-cleaned a portion of a highly decorated column that enframed the altar. The column was a prominent feature that the congregation faced each Sunday while listening to the sermon. The contrast between the restored and the unrestored fabric showed the parishioners what was possible. Nine months after the partially restored column was first revealed, the cathedral had raised the $8 million needed for a full restoration.

Using this as an example, Metro-North officials were persuaded to allow the restoration team to erect a scaffold platform suspended from a corner of the famous constellation ceiling of the Main Concourse. The location selected in the southeast corner made it possible for the restorers to be in contact with all the various parts of the ceiling: the painted surface of the cerulean blue sky, the gold leaf of the zodiac signs, the ornamental plaster of the rosettes covering the ventilation ducts behind the ceiling, the plaster surrounds to the clerestory windows, and the painted steel-framed windows. Balanced rather precariously on the

platform some hundred feet above the dashing commuters were the architects
and conservators experimenting with different cleaning and restoration techniques to use on the full ceiling.

The work platform was erected in the same manner in which an earlier
version had been built in 1944 to repair the original sky ceiling with a new surface and paint a new ceiling after the original 1913 version had been virtually
destroyed by water penetration in the 1930s. This work platform had been
ingeniously suspended from steel rods that passed through the surface of the
decorated ceiling and were bolted to the steel roof truss above the ceiling.

Under the direction of James W. Rhodes, the project's preservation director, with Dr. James Marston Fitch as their guide, and with the aid of some
extraordinary historical research by Deborah Rau, a team of conservators assembled. Jeff Greene from Evergreen Studios, Frank Welch, and Kinnery Silberman
test-cleaned various patches of the historic surfaces. Working at a small scale,
they developed conservation techniques that would be appropriate in the field.
In this manner we carefully developed the appropriate level of conservation for
all the surfaces, materials, and colors historically present.

The emphasis was on testing alternative methods for removing grime,
tobacco smoke, and fifty years of modern pollutants without removing the
original artwork. During this testing phase, the issue arose of which ceiling to
restore. Should the original 1913 sky mural be uncovered and revived or should
the 1944 mural remain and undergo restoration? As our mission was to reveal
the Terminal's original state, exposing the Main Concourse's first ceiling was an
exciting option until we discovered that its condition was so severely deteriorated that there was little left to restore. It was decided to restore the mural from
the 1940s, leaving the scant remains of the original ceiling undercover. Nevertheless, to demonstrate our commitment to restoration rather than replacement,
it was important for us to clean the mural without repainting it. If the various
experts could expose these materials and conditions, then there was a good
chance that we could develop sound and cost-effective conservation strategies
for all of the ceiling's individual parts.

Sometime after completing this experimental conservation work, a complex cleaning solution similar to the one used in the restoration of the Sistine
Chapel ceiling was identified as being the most appropriate. The conservators'
technical conclusion was that a nonabrasive conservator's wash would be effective
without losing or increasing the sheen or leaving any residue on the ceiling's mural.
Dimonium citrate (a chelating agent), sodium bicarbonate, and ammonium
bicarbonate were applied to the ceiling according to each area's unique condition.

The tests were carried out behind a shroud of black netting, enveloping
the work platform and giving the operation a sense of mystery. What *are* they
doing up there was the constant refrain. When the mysterious shroud and the
suspended platform were removed, a 75 foot long patch of restored ceiling was
revealed that looked so clean in contrast with the massive amount of unrestored
ceiling surrounding it that it appeared to be floodlit from some invisible source.

GRAND CENTRAL
TERMINAL

On any given day you could walk through the Main Concourse and hear the following debate: "Where's the light coming from?" "What do you mean, there's no light up there? Has to be, it's so bright."

The clean swatch of the constellation ceiling helped in raising money and saving money. Metro-North was awarded $2.8 million of federal funding for the restoration of the entire ceiling, and the experimental research and testing brought the original estimate of $14.6 million down to $4.2 million. By now the plan's successful completion appeared to depend on a patient blend of thinking and planning for the big picture while taking advantage of whatever funding sources were available to continue to show some forward movement.

The master plan was presented at a public hearing in April 1990. The overall cost of implementing this plan would be very high; approximately $425 million was the preliminary estimate for all its component parts. Of that, $135 million was proposed to come from MTA's capital program for 1992–96, $97 million from the 1997–2001 capital program, and $193 million to be funded from sources outside of MTA's capital programs. The following August the board approved a number of priority projects, including the restoration of the Waiting Room and the repair of the exterior cornice and the sculptural group by Jules-Alexis Coutan on the south facade. Starting with these first projects, each room

This rendering by Piyawat Pattanapuckdee illustrates Beyer Blinder Belle's vision of a rejuvenated Terminal and was used to help the design team win the Grand Central Terminal restoration project.
© Beyer Blinder Belle Architects & Planners

This section drawing, looking south, shows the new pedestrian passageways under Park Avenue that provide improved access and shorter travel times northbound from the Terminal.

Courtesy of MTA/Metro-North Collection

and space of Grand Central was returned to its most authentic state, incorporating as unobtrusively as possible new state-of-the-art technologies to equip the building.

To justify the level of expenditures from successive capital programs, the Metro-North leadership set about breaking down the budget totals into smaller packages focused toward first keeping the Terminal in a state of good repair (the Vanderbilt Avenue taxi stand and structural steel repairs were two of the earliest projects implemented in this category; later came the repair of the external cornice and sculptures on the south facade), and then improving and expanding system projects including major circulation improvements to the Lexington Avenue subway ramps, renamed the 42nd Street Passage.

From 1991 to 1994 we continued to work on aspects of the overall plan as funding became available. A companion document to the master plan was developed in 1992: a two-volume historic structures report, which recorded in greater detail the building's origins, history, changes over time, and existing conditions. This document played a vital role in enabling us to obtain the necessary approvals from the responsible public agencies and gain the vital support of the civic and historic preservation groups.

Fred Harris, then the director of the MTA's Real Estate Department, told his boss Stangl that though the master plan was comprehensive and insightful it contained no answers to the question of how to obtain the hundreds of millions of dollars necessary to carry out the restoration. He also pointed out that the plan did not identify any method by which the building could be legally protected from demolition or overbuilding should the legal battle be revived by the building's owners, Penn Central. He urged that these problems be addressed through the joint efforts of four legal entities: Metro-North, who would continue to operate the railroad and related support facilities; the MTA or a new MTA subsidiary to hold legal title to the Terminal; a not-for-profit corporation with a board of prominent New Yorkers committed to the preservation of the Terminal; and a for-profit corporation to provide a financing means in return for participation in future commercial revenues. The warning was that significant legal, political, and economic realities still needed to be addressed if the master plan was to have any chance of becoming a reality.

Harris's warnings to Stangl were well founded. The MTA did not have any ownership of the Terminal other than a lease that would expire in the year 2032 and that did not justify spending hundreds of millions of public dollars. And since Penn Central had been given the right to develop 1.8 million square feet of space by the 1978 Supreme Court decision, acquiring the Terminal with these development rights still attached to it would make the acquisition costs unaffordable.

The MTA's real estate lawyers set about working with the New York City Planning Department to create a Grand Central special district within the boundaries of which the Terminal's available development rights could be transferred. After months of negotiation and public hearings in the spring of 1992, city-sponsored legislation was passed and the MTA acquired a 110-year lease on the terminal building. In 1994, six years after the project was awarded, the go-ahead to implement the master plan was given by the MTA.

As the project began to build momentum, Peter Stangl

Restoration included such intricacies as regilding the elaborate clock and repairing the colorful Tiffany glass clock face, located at the center of the sculptural group.

Courtesy of MTA/Metro-North Collection, Frank English photographer

A complex assemblage of scaffolding wrapped the Indiana limestone sculpture group atop the 42nd Street facade. Architects, conservators, and craftspeople worked from the platforms revitalizing the splendor of Jules-Alexis Coutan's massive work of art.

© Beyer Blinder Belle Architects & Planners, James W. Rhodes photographer

was promoted from president of Metro-North to chairman of the MTA. In addition to overseeing the continued progress of Metro-North, he now had the responsibility of doing the same for all the other divisions of the MTA. He knew that in order to keep the Grand Central restoration moving forward, he would need someone not distracted by other responsibilities to give full-time attention to the project. He promoted Vice President Donald Nelson, a known and respected "railroad man," to president of Metro-North, thus ensuring that the progress in increased ridership and better service would continue. Also, reaching out to the private sector, he appointed Susan Fine to be the MTA's director of real estate with the primary responsibility of completing Grand Central's restoration. As the real estate development cycle of the 1980s slowed to a standstill in the early 1990s, talented people like Fine became available to bring the innovations of the private sector into the public arena—especially skills needed to curb the cost overruns to which large public projects were susceptible. Some of the project's administrators were concerned that Fine's aggressive, private sector leadership style would not foster a bond between the public

and private sectors. But Fine knew that without strong leadership in a project with such a large and diverse number of players, with their own agendas, the project could come to a standstill.

By now, the time was ripe for the merger of the public and private worlds. The intense battles to save Grand Central Terminal during the 1960s and 1970s had pitted private sector interests—the Penn Central Railroad and its developers UGP Properties—against the public sector and civic groups—New York City and the Municipal Art Society. In the 1990s it seemed the perfect cathartic healing process for the actual restoration to move forward under the banner of a public-private partnership.

For politicians and public administrators, the public-private partnership was a useful vehicle for building large-scale projects at a time when traditional public funding sources were drying up. For private sector developers and real estate investors, it offered them access to publicly indemnified financing, thus reducing or eliminating risk in exchange for greater public scrutiny and accountability. In the often tough approval process it also helped to have as a partner an agency responsible for protecting the public interest. And civic and community groups believed that such public-private partnerships were more responsive and accountable than either party was individually.

Williams Jackson Ewing Inc., who had originally been hired in 1988 as retail marketing consultants, formed a joint venture partnership with LaSalle Partners called GCTVenture to lease, construct, and manage the restoration plan, which was now renamed the Grand Central Revitalization Plan. This partnership team had been extremely successful in the rebirth of Washington's Union Station. The architects working with this now expanded cast prepared a somewhat scaled-down but achievable plan based on realistic funding sources, but a problem arose. The MTA had neglected to require that GCTVenture invest financially in the project; this created a major disincentive to the efficient execution of the restoration plan. With no capital at risk, GCTVenture moved no faster or decisively than a public sector agency would. Worse yet, when different agendas surfaced between the MTA and Metro-North, GCTVenture did not have the financial muscle to intervene and resolve these conflicts.

In March 1994, the MTA entered into an agreement with GCTVenture that would form the basis for implementing the modified master plan: the Grand Central Terminal Revitalization Plan, the $200 million program completed in 1999. A key component of the plan was that, by increasing the revenue stream from an expanded retail component, substantial private funding could be attracted to the project. Specifically, it was anticipated that the retail rent roll, which expanded from $6 million to $13 million per year, would provide the income to pay off an $84 million construction bond that was successfully sold on the Wall Street bond market.

In 1995, with a new five-year capital program funded by the state and the construction bond secured by private financing, Stangl moved on after twenty-

Demolition begins to reveal the scale of the original Oyster Bar ramps before they were reduced to an insignificant low-ceilinged space when the Ticket Office extensions were built in 1927.

© James Rudnick Photography

five years of public service to become president of Bombardier Transit Corp. Standing in the restored Waiting Room bidding him farewell was a bittersweet moment for us. We wondered how we could continue without the man who had been the patriarch of the restoration project. Great progress had been made and the glittering chandeliers above us were living proof, but with so much more to do how were we to achieve this without his inspired leadership? After Stangl's departure, Don Nelson, especially, held things together amid changes that could have derailed the entire project. Susan Fine, after three years as the point person for Stangl, left her position as MTA's director of real estate to rejoin the private sector as part of the Tishman Speyer Rockefeller Center team. Following George Pataki's election as governor in the fall of 1994, his new appointees moved into leadership positions at the MTA with different goals for the project.

The changing of the guard came at a time when construction was beginning to pick up momentum. Under any circumstances this would be a difficult time in a project. As pressure builds to complete the building, time and money are under intensive scrutiny and it is difficult for the client and the architect not to compromise either quality or the original intent and risk criticism for cost overruns or completion delays. It is at this point, whether in the public or the private sector, that strong wills are needed to hold on to the project's goals and integrity.

**The original grand scale of the
Oyster Bar ramps begins to reveal
itself through a forest of scaffolds.**
© James Rudnick Photography

This sensitive issue of maintaining the quality of the plan's original intentions was greatly aggravated by the lack of continuity of personnel working on
almost every aspect of the project. With the exception of Williams Jackson
Ewing's key leasing staff and the architects' and engineers' staff, very few of
the personnel originally assigned from either the public or the private sector
remained involved with the project. The private sector project managers with
no equity stake had little or no incentive to aggressively manage the contractor.
The newly appointed public sector administrators pushed aside the Metro-
North personnel who had considerable knowledge and commitment to both
the railroad and the Terminal. And the general contractor never assigned to the
project the preservation project manager who attended the job interview for
selection, replacing her as soon as they were awarded the project.

The project proceeded in this way for the final three years of construction, with constant confrontations about the quality of the project between the
architects in the field and the managers for both GCTVenture and the contractors. Ironically, the situation was not helped by the presence in the field of a
fully staffed architect's office. Years of working on similar restoration had taught
us that a faithful interpretation of our plans was best achieved by having a full
staff of architects and engineers present on the job site. Douglas McKean, one
of Beyer Blinder Belle's second-generation leaders dedicated to the challenges
of historic preservation, directed a core field team including Don Fiorino, who
had been through a similar experience with Ellis Island; Mark Nusbaum, who

had worked on restoration projects at Yale University; Frank Prial, Jr., who had prior transportation experience at Kennedy Airport; and Jean Campbell, who had critical retail experience. Unfortunately, the field office was too accessible to the construction managers, who were quick to accuse the architects and engineers of not providing them with information vital to the construction and slow to review the drawings that contained the answers to their questions. A certain amount of this posturing goes on in all projects, but it was particularly acute on this one because of the leadership vacuum.

The restoration process took on the nature of a theatrical, and sometimes positively operatic, production. There was a huge cast, often performing multiple roles in the restoration. And there was the building's audience, the everyday users, putting up with constant changes to their favorite routes and departures platforms, watching with growing interest the changes to a building that was as much a part of their lives as lunch or a paycheck. Given that half a million people saw this show every day, their opinions would be the ones that counted.

CHAPTER NINE

GRAND CENTRAL IS REBORN

Once more a great railroad station.
—PETER STANGL

The foundation for the successful restoration of an historic building is the passionate and relentless pursuit to understand the original architect's intentions. We must transport ourselves back in time to fully understand how the building was originally conceived, how this differed from its implementation, and what changes occurred over the years since its original construction. Only then can an appropriate plan to restore and update a building be proposed.

This was the first goal we dedicated ourselves to as we began to prepare the master plan. It was a twofold investigation. The first part was a physical inspection of every nook and cranny of the building itself; the second part was research into the building's archives and all documentation in original drawings, photographs, sketches, notebooks, letters, memos, newspaper accounts, books, and any other source that would give us clues to the building's origins, shape, and purpose. This type of search is always a combination of anticipation and tedium. Like detective work, it combines many hours of sifting through meaningless dirt for a few nuggets of pure gold.

When we started our master planning adventure we set up shop high above the Terminal's Main Concourse in a small suite of rundown offices. Hall B 4th Floor became home to a small group of architects and engineers intent on learning everything about Grand Central by crawling all over the building and making daily sorties to a space full of old drawings and documents in Grand Central's Plan Room. Here we were to strike gold several times but not always to realize it until later. Here we found the original drawings by Warren & Wetmore showing the unbuilt east staircase, and here Charles Kramer, one of the project architects, found the remarkable evidence that the Oyster Bar ramps had not always had low ceilings. James Rhodes still remembers the sight of Charlie running across the great glass window wall with a roll of drawings under his arm like a man who has just found the holy grail. To find solid evidence of the original

A fiery glow radiates from the steel truss that moves across the sky ceiling as conservators restore its original brilliance.
© James Rudnick Photography

architects' intent such as the unbuilt stair or the height of the Oyster Bar ramps was more than an act of discovery. It was crucial to substantiating the incorporation of these features into a seventy-five-year-old building and receiving the approvals necessary from the preservation, state, and city agencies.

We organized ourselves into four teams, each responsible for a different aspect of the building. Through searching the archives in the Plan Room and other sources such as Columbia University's Avery Library, the New-York Historical Society, the New York Public Library, and the files and records of the railroad companies, a great deal of information was revealed. In the Plan Room we discovered approximately 18,000 drawings, including the original Warren & Wetmore ink-on-linen drawings. We inspected this vast collection and selected about 2,000 drawings with sufficiently useful information that we copied and placed into our computer files. "We had photographs, drawings of various sizes and condition," noted Robert McMillan, a senior technical architect on the project. "Each of these documents had to be addressed as to whether it was applicable to the building's current conditions." It was from that collection that we culled our 2,000 drawings and made duplicates with the understanding that some would be archived for later years in print or photographic medium. The second level of intervention was to take an original drawing or one that was sufficiently articulated and have it scanned into the computer. It required a considerable amount of digital redrafting of the original documents in order to bring them to a level of accuracy and usability in the recording of existing conditions. Some of these drawings, while appearing initially to be only of peripheral interest, provided us with some of our most valuable insights. For example, the set of original plumbing drawings gave us the most accurate information about conditions *behind* many of the building's walls, saving us the time and expense of having to open up walls in order to obtain the same information.

At the same time that the team was examining the treasures of the Plan Room, we were also becoming very familiar with the building itself, crawling, climbing, descending, and ascending to learn its secrets, from the subterranean passage 90 feet below street level, known as Burma Road, to the attic space between the recently repaired roof and the sky ceiling, some 100 feet above the Concourse floor.

Our purpose was twofold: to inspect up close the existing conditions of the building's fabric and to verify that what was represented on those 2,000 drawings matched the actual physical conditions. "Field checking" the existing documentation often reveals differences; if one relied solely on the drawings, the architects and engineers who would be preparing a new set of construction drawings could get an inaccurate picture of the actual existing conditions.

The more research we did, the more apparent it became that in order to bring the building back to its original glory we would have to combine the architects' original vision with the needs of a railroad for the twenty-first century. What made Grand Central such an extraordinary building originally still held true. It was and is a "mixing valve" of receiving and dispersing huge numbers of

An important discovery during our research of existing drawings, this 1911 Warren & Wetmore drawing of the Main Concourse illustrates the architect's original intention. It includes two matching single-flight staircases at each end of the concourse. Also shown is the skylight that would bring light into the Terminal from the light well of the twenty-story office building above the Terminal.

Avery Architectural and Fine Arts Library, Columbia University in the City of New York

people every day in a pattern of clear circulation paths in all directions—both horizontally and vertically. Because of this clear circulation system of ramps, stairs, and elevated roadways there were no collisions and no confusion.

In the first forty years of the Terminal's life it served three distinctly separate needs: the long-distance incoming traffic, the long-distance outgoing traffic (both on the Main Concourse level), and the suburban traffic (on the lower level). Since the Terminal's usage has changed to handle regional traffic only, the three separate traffic patterns had to be fused to form a single circulation system. The challenge was to create a new pattern of circulation, still without collision and confusion, that would bring together all the brilliant features of the original. The boldest elements of the original 1990 master plan focused on introducing new circulation elements into the Terminal. A three-story-high Galleria was proposed as Grand Central's new portal to Lexington Avenue and east midtown (when Grand Central Terminal was first built there was no need to have an approach in this direction, since nothing but rail yards and slaughterhouses existed there). This $40 million feature would be radically modified by the 1994 revised development plan.

To visually reinforce the train operations that the main and lower concourses now shared, new escalators were originally proposed to be set into 40 foot by 40 foot openings in the Main Concourse's floor immediately under the east and west balconies. Estimated to cost $12 million, these large openings were eliminated when a cost-benefit analysis concluded that the same operational benefits would be accomplished by the escalators being constructed without the large openings.

While the sense of people hurrying in all directions was the essence of Grand Central, circulation across a newly restored Main Concourse should be as generous, unencumbered, clear, and accommodating as possible. The aim was to make sure that all New Yorkers believed that *the* indoor city meeting space was by the gold clock in the middle of the Main Concourse, where once again all routes through the Terminal would clearly converge. So as well as building new circulation paths, we set about closing down the outdated passageways and removing all the accretions that distracted from the Terminal's basic circulation pattern. Once again, travelers are drawn into the heart of a restored Concourse where the great Tennessee marble floor lies like a lake under a blue sky with a gilded constellation to guide them on their journey.

New escalators on the east and west sides of the Terminal link the lower concourse to the upper concourse, improving the circulation between the two train levels that now serve as a single railroad station.

Rendering © Beyer Blinder Belle Architects & Planners/Architectural Delineator: Porto Folio Inc.; photograph © Peter Aaron/Esto

Originally, the Waiting Room to the south of the Main Concourse was a peaceful place for passengers to relax and wait. By 1989, no longer serving the commuter-traveler in that manner, it had become a shelter for the homeless and a harsh reminder of the city outside its walls.

The original rich palette of materials had grown bleak. The Caen stone walls were stained and broken, the Bottocino marble and the Tennessee pink marble floors were cracked and chipped, and the ornamental plasterwork was encrusted with thick layers of grime. The decorative metalwork that had once made the room sparkle was barely visible, painted a dreary dark brown. All this was seen by the architects and conservators not as daunting but rather as a wonderful opportunity to turn a sow's ear into a silk purse. It would also be a self-contained laboratory to test techniques of cleaning and restoration that could be used for the larger part of the building. In the winter of 1990, we began to bring the Waiting Room back to life.

Conservation and restoration techniques were developed to renew the historic marbles, hardwoods, ornamental plaster and limestone, metal windows, doors and grilles and the sixteen-foot-high decorative chandeliers that hung from the ceiling. Early efforts began by erecting scaffolds to permit close examination of the ceiling and walls and to test a variety of conservation technologies, some conventional and some experimental.

Up on the scaffold the wired glass in the great arched windows appeared for the first time to be quite different from contemporary wired glass, which is somewhat coarser and more industrial. Not enough of the historic glass could be salvaged to replace all the cracked and broken panes, but through extensive research, a "sparrow" wire was discovered that could be custom woven in Belgium.

By the early 1980s the stately Waiting Room, like the rest of the Terminal, was overcommercialized and poorly maintained.

© Beyer Blinder Belle Architects & Planners

When this was laminated into glass, it became a close match to the delicate historic wired glass.

The five great chandeliers were carefully lowered and dismantled before being shipped off to a restoration workshop in Salt Lake City that had the expertise to deal with the intricate blend of metals. Taking advantage of the need to dismantle the chandeliers, the team studied ways in which to insert unobtrusively additional light fixtures into the center. When the chandeliers were reinstalled, they could serve both their traditional function and modern requirements of greater wattage in public spaces. Reinstalled ten months after they were removed, the contrast between their previous drab, dull, bronze-like color and the refurbished and replated nickel and gold was spectacular. In their newly restored form they were suspended below a coffered, ornamental, plaster ceiling recently repaired and transformed from a dark nicotine brown to a warm sand color.

Scaffolding fills the Waiting Room as the Caen stone walls, plaster details, marble floor, and chandeliers undergo extensive restoration.

© Beyer Blinder Belle Architects & Planners, James W. Rhodes photographer

Paint systems were tested and adjusted to arrive at a color for the room's ornamental metal window frames that matched the original soft gray green. Sources of Bottocino marble were discovered, slightly deeper in hue and veined more closely than the historic marble, but ultimately close enough to make a match. The restoration of the Tennessee pink marble floor was more difficult; though we did not know it at the time, this would prove to be the material most difficult to match throughout the entire restoration campaign.

Heavy oak benches around the perimeter of the room were restored, iron doorway frames were replicated, and grilles for heating and cooling systems were refinished. The stone portal centered on the east wall was reopened, and the marble panels on either side of it were restored. New marble dadoes were installed and the badly shattered Roman travertine ramp leading to the Main Concourse was replaced with new travertine.

Yet none of these careful and discrete restoration efforts would have their full impact without the cleaning of the seventy-foot-high artificial Caen stone walls, which over the years had become encased in grime from the air pollution of the railroad's daily operation. Artificial Caen stone, made to imitate limestone, is actually a fibrous plaster-like mixture of crushed limestone, gravel, lime, Portland cement, plaster, and sand. The team knew from previous experience that to attempt to use one of the most common cleaning techniques of applying water or steam through a high-pressure system on this material would simply drive the grimy particles deeper into the stone's pores. Instead, the architects took the beauty salon approach and gave the grand old lady a facial. Conservators prepared a solution that consisted of liquid ammoniated latex rubber and painted it onto the walls. Left to cure overnight, in the morning it was peeled from the walls, like a facial mask, bringing with it years of aging and dirt. The Waiting Room was left with warm sandstone-colored walls just as in 1913.

After eighteen months of intense focused efforts by the team, the Waiting Room was transformed into a setting suitable for a series of cultural and commercial events: a reception for the 1992 Democratic National Convention, a gala for the Municipal Art Society, an exhibit by the artist Red Grooms, two popular seasonal bazaars, and a somber and dignified memorial for the passing of Jacqueline Kennedy Onassis.

One of the first major events in the restored Waiting Room was the reception for then Governor Bill Clinton during the 1992 Democratic National Convention in New York.
Courtesy of MTA/Metro-North Collection, Frank English photographer

One of the first steps in saving an old building from ultimate collapse is to fix the roof or, to reinterpret the old horseman's saying of "no hoof, no horse," "no roof, no building." Though Metro-North had repaired the roof, the effect of the water damage was still visible. The walls of Bottocino marble and Caen stone rising up to meet the ornamental plaster cornices and painted plaster ceilings were cracking, spalling, and badly stained. Their surfaces had grayed from the residue of a former unoriginal finish and accumulations of years of soot and grime.

The windows on the north balcony of the Concourse had been painted over in the 1960s when the Pan Am Building was built. Throughout the Concourse the color of the metal windows and ornamental ironwork was a dreary brown, not the original light olive green that had simulated the color of patinated bronze. Behind the walls much of the steel had rusted to the point where it needed replacing. The lighting was extremely poor, which was something of a blessing, since its dim effect helped to visually minimize these conditions. The surfaces had not been maintained for many years. The Kodak sign; the Newsweek clock; the ticker-tape booth; the tall, inappropriate, and out-of-scale train indicator boards were all aesthetically at war with one another. The overall impression was that of a tired, sad building gradually wrapped in layer upon layer of shabby clothing. Using the invaluable experiences gained during the restoration of the Waiting Room, we set about cataloging the conditions and refining our restoration techniques. But in addition to restoring those materials also found in the Waiting Room, there was one additional unique challenge: the sky ceiling.

Warren & Wetmore had originally designed a glazed lantern skylight to occupy most of the ceiling. The idea was abandoned late in the evolution of the Terminal's design, and when the lantern skylight design was replaced with the sky ceiling it was done as a collaboration between architect and artist. Whitney

A solution of ammonia and liquidized rubber is applied to the Caen stone walls that when partially dry is peeled off, lifting the years of dirt and grime.

Above: © James Rudnick Photography; Right: © Beyer Blinder Belle Architects & Planners, James W. Rhodes photographer

Warren conceived the astronomical mural; his colleague Paul Helleu contributed to it and added the idea of illuminating the major stars. J. Monroe Hewlett, an architect and muralist, developed the design and detailed cartoons, and the actual painting was executed by Charles Basing and the Hewlett-Basing Studio. The ceiling opened to rave reviews even though Hewlett and Basing had chosen artistic license over scientific accuracy.

The original painting, done with egg tempura on the plaster ceiling, was by the late 1920s beginning to deteriorate due to roof leaks. By the early 1940s little was left. In 1944 the mural was scraped, plaster repaired, and a new surface made of four-foot by eight-foot boards cemented and stapled over the original ceiling. The project was led by Charles Gulbrandsen, who was an apprentice in the Hewlett-Basing Studio when the first ceiling was created. It was this surface, the second version of the sky ceiling, that we restored. In 1990, the team examined this ceiling, accompanied by Gulbrandsen's grandson, a painter and muralist.

When it came time to restore the entire ceiling, a twenty-eight-foot-wide bridge of aluminum and wood spanned the width of the Main Concourse. It was constructed to slide on runners laid on top of the cornice from which the sky ceiling sprang. During the course of the sky ceiling restoration, the truss would move twenty-five feet at a time, from one end of the sky ceiling to the other, allowing John Canning's team of conservators to clean every detail of the heavens.

As full-scale restoration begins, the walls of the Main Concourse are covered with scaffolding and protective drapes.
© James Rudnick Photography

Behind the drapes, the heavily detailed entablature of the Main Concourse is restored.
© James Rudnick Photography

The sky ceiling's restoration happened high above the heads of the Terminal's users, fully visible to them every day for nine months. It was a tangible way to measure our slow but steady accomplishments. Even the most seasoned commuters couldn't resist walking across the marble floor with heads tilted backward, staring heavenward in disbelief. The drama between the two halves—restored and unrestored—captivated them. As more of the ceiling became visible to the commuters on the Main Concourse it looked as if the sun had broken through a dark cloud.

An important part of the ceiling's restoration included cleaning and restoring the ornamental plaster surrounding the sky mural. These intricate rosettes, with decorative motifs of acorns and oak leaves, were fondly referred to by the architects and conservators as Grand Central's "secret garden." And

**More than one hundred feet above
the Main Concourse floor, the
rosettes that border the sky ceiling
are restored to their original beauty.**
© James Rudnick Photography

One of the ceiling's 2,500 stars in a before-and-after state.

© James Rudnick Photography

A member of John Canning's ceiling restoration team applies the chemical solution, working across the vast ceiling.

Opposite:

Following the equinox of the sky ceiling from west to east, the restoration of the Main Concourse progresses. Behind barriers, the steel of the east stair is being laid and the information booth is being restored. The north and south sides of the concourse are rediscovering their original grandeur behind construction drapes that are covered with commercial messages.

© James Rudnick Photography

though innovative and sophisticated techniques are often used in building conservation, sometimes what works best is something simple—perhaps even something that can be found in one's own home. The first stage of the rosette restoration began with vacuuming the buildup of grime from the highly ornamental plasterwork that surrounded the vents. Next the rosettes were cleaned with a gentle soap-and-water solution. Finally, they were repainted with a warm, creamy off-white color.

When the entire ceiling work was completed, it revealed the original, somewhat startling blue-green mural and the gold-leaf zodiacal signs and ten constellations that had been restored and rerendered in twenty-four-karat gold leaf. Sixty of the major stars were illuminated by tiny lights, using a high-tech system of fiber optics. The mural's purpose in 1913 was to help create an enriched environment that could not be produced by architecture alone. That remains as true today as it did then.

Restoring the brass clock that marks the popular meeting place at the information booth.

© James Rudnick Photography

Buildings designated as landmarks often have distinguishing features that are quite different from their designers' original intentions. Ten years of design and construction inevitably meant that the Terminal went through a number of changes to its original plans. One of the most radical of these was the elimination of a twenty-story office building that was to have been built immediately above the ceiling of the Main Concourse.

Drawings dating from 1911 show a bulky, squat building sitting atop the Terminal. Elevators and stair towers to serve these offices were placed at the four corners of the Concourse. In order not to conflict with the railroad tracks running below, these towers stopped at the balcony level of the terminal. And in the original plans grand ornamental staircases were designed to link the two train concourses to the balcony level from which elevators and stairs would ascend to twenty stories of offices.

If this had been built, the ceiling of the Main Concourse would have had a great glazed lantern skylight looking up into the court of the office building above. The grand staircases leading to the balcony "sky lobbies" were depicted in a rendering dated 1911 as a single sweeping flight of stairs unbroken by landings or directional changes. But as construction of the office building grew closer, the real estate market went into a downturn and the building was abandoned. However, by this point the elevator banks and stair towers had already been built up to the highest floor within the Main Concourse.

The east end of the Main Concourse, once a baggage check counter, then a bank, is stripped and opened to make way for the new east stair.

© James Rudnick Photography

The two monumental staircases Whitney Warren planned as part of the office building design were at the east and west ends of the Main Concourse. With the removal of the office building from the plans, the east staircase was abandoned completely and the west staircase was modified from a single sweeping flight to the staircase we are familiar with today. Despite the significant loss of symmetry through the disappearance of the east staircase, Warren had the opportunity to rethink the design of the remaining staircase on the west side of the Main Concourse. With Charles Garnier's design of the grand stair in the Paris Opera as an important inspiration, Warren developed the design that still exists today. In both the Opera and the Terminal the staircase guides users from level to level by a series of short flights of stairs, each of which offers a different view of the Concourse below.

The loss of the matching staircase gave the Concourse a strangely unbalanced look, as if a limb had been amputated from an otherwise perfectly formed human body. Despite its prominent position, the East Balcony was not easily accessible. It ended up being used predominantly for displays for tourism, the Bremen airplane, the first plane to cross the North Atlantic from east to west, and the Kodak sign. The vertical circulation linking the lower to the main concourse also suffered from this lack of architectural symmetry, especially after long-distance service abandoned Grand Central for Penn Station and the two concourses needed to function as one.

Although our research had uncovered substantiated facts about the building's design, any changes to original, historic fabric are considered by preservationists suspiciously. The preservationist's point of view was that no change could be an improvement to the original. It is a justifiable position when one looks at so many insensitive "interventions" by contemporary architects who in the name of progress have radically changed the appearance of historic buildings using inappropriate designs or materials.

To understand the preservationist's level of concern, one must look at both the differences and similarities between architects practicing in the field of historic preservation and historians or preservationists not trained as architects. Architects see themselves as instruments of change who take the position that buildings should continue to exist only if society has a use for them. And though most building changes over time are in response to changing social, cultural, and economic conditions, the architect's mission sometimes puts them in conflict with others in the preservation field. The preservationist's point of view, on the other hand, begins with the belief that an artifact is best preserved in its original state.

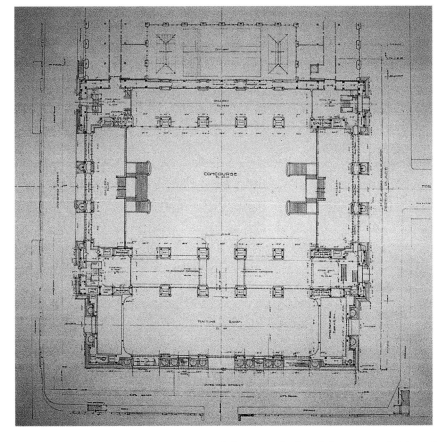

An original plan prepared by Warren & Wetmore showing two identical staircases at the eastern and western ends of the Main Concourse.
Courtesy of MTA/Metro-North Collection

Over time the professional debate between preservation architects and other preservationists, historians, and reviewing agencies has been an intense one. The preservationists' concerns are not unwarranted. It used to be that most architects had no interest and little professional training in the research activities that we spent so much time on in the early days of Grand Central's restoration. Therefore, more often than not, architects' proposals for the restoration of a historic building were not well informed by research of its past, and the changes that had taken place over time were not fully researched and documented. Too often the change or modification proposed was wholly inappropriate, being ignorant of and insensitive toward the building's historic fabric and origins.

Nowadays, the areas of preservation and restoration have grown immensely in the architectural profession. Many architects are formally educated and trained in the discipline of historic preservation. As part of that training they have learned the importance of research and the relationship between architectural scholarship and architectural practice. They have learned that stewardship is as important as design intervention and that their own design ideas must

first respect the intent of the building's original authors. These advances in
architectural thinking and practice ensure that the best architects working in the
field today have the same desire to understand their subject's origins, history,
and morphological growth as do their historic preservationist colleagues who
are not architects.

The result is that the ongoing discussion between architect (instrument
of change) and preservationist (all change is inferior to the original) is a far more
equal debate. There are prejudices remaining that reflect the different objectives
of each camp, but no longer is the architect the barbarian at the gate and the
historian the keeper of the flame. Sometimes the architect must be forgiven for
wondering if he is being damned for his proposals of change or envied for his
knowledgeable research.

At Grand Central, our careful researching of all available sources uncovered an original drawing by Warren & Wetmore showing a plan view of the stair

**The opening has been made and
the new steel is delivered for the
structure of the stairway.**

Photographs this page: © James Rudnick
Photography

The steel structure is covered with marble by the masons as the stair nears completion.

© James Rudnick Photography

After eighty-five years of existing only on architectural drawings, the east stair is complete.

© James Rudnick Photography

originally designed for the East Balcony. With it we could demonstrate to our colleagues on the city and state historic commissions that the idea of such a staircase was not an ego-driven ploy to have our personal imprint on the building, but that in fact our goal was to complete the original design. Why would we turn away from giving the building back the one missing element to Warren's intended symmetry? Thus began months of sometimes volatile debate on what the appropriate staircase was to insert in this grand space.

The initial proposal combined two ideas: first, to construct the missing east stair as originally designed by Warren, and second to surround the east and west stairs with large openings in the floor of the Main Concourse. Our intent was to improve the visibility between the main and lower concourses, since they now operate in concert. But this proposal was such a drastic change for the preservationists, and so expensive for the MTA, that we retreated to consider other more modest proposals.

There were many opinions about what the unbuilt staircase should look like. Some argued that it should be a contemporary interpretation of the original design—modern (i.e., smaller) versus historic (i.e., grander). To others a staircase built in the 1990s should be deliberately different from the plan of the original, with distinctively different materials than the existing historic Vanderbilt Avenue staircase—perhaps metal rather than marble. On and on the debate went, with

The restoration of the Main
Concourse nears completion.

© James Rudnick Photography

the architects drawing many of these ideas for review even though some were pretty awful. There was no doubt in our minds that the best solution was to build the staircase as closely as possible to Warren & Wetmore's original idea, adding small changes to reflect changes in the quarrying and the finishing of marble due to today's technology. In this manner the new staircase would signal to the contemporary viewer that it was built at the end of the twentieth century and not at the beginning. But Grand Central is everybody's building and there were many parties involved with different agendas and constituencies to serve. The MTA's operating arm, Metro-North, did not want to be criticized for spending public funds unnecessarily on lavish architectural features; the leasing arm of the private developer worried about how the staircase would impact the use of the east balcony by a restaurant tenant; and the public reviewing agencies fretted about the new staircase not being mistaken in the future for a staircase that had existed since the Terminal's beginnings in 1913. The public reviewing agencies also showed great sensitivity to there being adequate public access to the balconies via the staircase.

Every week there was another meeting about the staircase, more concerns, and a host of new solutions. At one point the architect in charge accused a senior public official of wasting time and money by pursuing any and all solutions regardless of merit; in return he was accused of being stubborn and inflexible. A screaming match ensued that cleared the air and allowed work to continue. Everyone agreed that the architects should prepare drawings and models that reflected the original staircase design. Michael Wetstone, a young designer at Beyer Blinder Belle, eagerly took on the assignment of preparing beautiful drawings detailing every aspect of the staircase.

Just as the Waiting Room had been a laboratory for the rest of the building, the staircase became a trial that illustrated the many changes the Terminal would need to go through in order to function as well in the twenty-first century as it has in this century. When the east staircase was unveiled to the public in October 1998, people saw Warren's original design with a few small changes to the balustrades that in their simple modern details would signal to future visitors that the stair was built eighty-six years after first being designed and using late-twentieth-century technology.

As the Beaux Arts style of Grand Central is directly traceable to Whitney Warren's authorship, the extensive system of ramps that connect the Terminal to the street and the express to the suburban levels are clearly attributable to Charles Reed's hand. From the early days of planning, the Terminal's designers—particularly Reed—realized that if the two levels of railroad tracks were each to be serviced by their own pedestrian concourse, then the connections between them and the streets surrounding the Terminal should be as seamless as possible. Despite many changes between 1903 and 1913, when the Terminal was finished, this powerful concept of people moving prevailed and became an essential part of Grand Central's fluid brilliance. But over the years, some major visual modifications in

the vicinity of the ramps compromised the clarity of the building's circulation.

The Oyster Bar ramps—so-called because their base is located at the Oyster Bar and Restaurant—were originally constructed as a space that soared approximately 90 feet high with five great chandeliers floating in the magnificent volume to mirror an identical set of five chandeliers placed over the north balcony on the opposite side of the Main Concourse. But in 1927, as the rail traveling habits of the nation were skyrocketing, the railroad operators decided that the only way to accommodate the burgeoning needs was to bridge over this high space of the ramps with more and larger ticket offices. The 90-foot-high space was lowered to a confining passageway leading down to the lower concourse, a space that became an unwelcoming destination. In fact, it became so unwelcoming that Metro-North was forced to close the lower concourse at night.

In the 1990s, with different travel habits and ticketing technology, the space needed for extra ticket offices had been greatly mitigated. Just as we did with the east staircase, we went before our constituents, peers, and government agencies and stated the case for reopening the space and enabling the Oyster Bar ramps beneath to regain their lofty height. The idea was approved by the Landmarks Preservation Commission and the space has become one of the Terminal's most visually exciting. New Bottocino marble and Caen stone line the walls; a new walking surface has replaced the worn-out portions of the original ramps; and one new feature has been added. Originally as part of the "three stations in

The new restored Main Concourse in a rare moment of silence.

© James Rudnick Photography

one" concept, an eight-foot-high wall acted as a visual barrier between the long-distance travelers moving from Waiting Room to the Main Concourse's train gates on the upper level and the suburban travelers using the Oyster Bar ramps, crossing below. We have chosen not to reinstall this wall, and in its place there is now a simple, waist-high balustrade that allows people on both levels to see one another moving through the terminal.

The Vanderbilt Avenue ramp had also gone through some compromising changes over the years. When the Terminal opened in 1913, the entry at the corner of Vanderbilt Avenue and 42nd Street had a distinctive wrought iron–framed glass canopy that led into a hall at the top of a high, broad passageway. Immediately inside the entrance a ramp led down to the Main Concourse level. This too was Reed's genius at work, making travelers welcome and immediately propelling them down an attractive broad ramp into the heart of the building. However, this attractive volume of air space above the ramp became a popular ladies shoe store, Kitty Kelly, giving the ramp its familiar name, the Kitty Kelly ramp. In more recent times the space was occupied by Federal Express. Federal Express has been removed and once again the restored entrance ramp attracts users into the Terminal in the manner Reed intended.

From 1927 to 1998, the Oyster Bar ramps to the suburban level were covered by the expanded ticket office facilities.

© Beyer Blinder Belle Architects & Planners, Anne Edris photographer

The chandeliers have been returned from their restoration in Salt Lake City, Utah, and are being raised back over the Oyster Bar ramps. Each chandelier weighs 2,500 pounds, measures 11 feet across, and holds 144 exposed lightbulbs. The original appearance of bronze, gold plating, and nickel has been restored.

© James Rudnick Photography

The balustraded bridge above the arch is a new feature that replaces an eight-foot-high solid wall that originally created a visual barrier between travelers on both levels.

© James Rudnick Photography

Opposite: A construction shot of the Oyster Bar ramps: the chandeliers have been removed for restoration, the floors of the expanded ticket booths have been removed, and the space is beginning to reveal its original scale.

© James Rudnick Photography

The ramp at the corner of 42nd Street and Vanderbilt Avenue was restricted by adjoining retail stores.
© Beyer Blinder Belle Architects & Planners, Anne Edris photographer

In this drawing, Charles Reed's original, spacious ramp system is restored. Not only are the passages and storefronts of the lower level visible, but the Vanderbilt Avenue taxi stand can be seen through the glass.
© Beyer Blinder Belle Architects & Planners/Architectural Delineator: Porto Folio Inc.

Given that the Terminal covers over 200,000 square feet at grade level, it was inevitable that it would be developed with a series of passageways leading from the core out to the surrounding streets. In some instances these passageways were actually portions of neighboring buildings on the street level. The Graybar Passage, which leads out from the Main Concourse to Lexington Avenue, north of 43rd Street, is actually part of the ground floor of the Graybar Building, a 30-story office tower built in 1927. Similarly, the passageway on the south side of 43rd Street was originally called the Commodore Passage, being within the ground floor of the original Commodore Hotel. In the 1970s when this hotel was renamed the Grand Hyatt, the passage followed suit. Now it has been renamed the Lexington Passage. Both of these passages have been restored and given new retail identities. The Graybar has services such as shoe repair, film

The restored Vanderbilt Avenue ramp connects the street level to the Main Concourse. Through the windows above the ramp is the reactivated, covered Vanderbilt taxi stand.

© Peter Aaron/Esto

developing, and a wine store, and the Lexington has small boutique gift shops similar to a European arcade.

In between these two historic passageways is a new route located on the original roadbed of 43rd Street and the site of the Terminal's original offstreet service dock as well as a former bank. This is the 43rd Street Market, a 44-foot-wide new entrance leading into the heart of the Terminal from Lexington Avenue, giving the Terminal its own dedicated entrance from the east for the first time in its history. On the western side of the Terminal, where separate parts of the Terminal originally had been connected to the crosstown shuttle subway line by two passages, a single wide passageway now links the entire Terminal to the shuttle.

The Terminal's main connection with the Lexington Avenue subway line—the 42nd Street Passage—was widened to accommodate the greatly increased pedestrian flow. New underground passageways beneath the sidewalks on both sides of Park Avenue from 48th Street to the Main Concourse—the North End Access system—give commuters more convenient ways to move north and south. Building on the distinctive features of Reed's original ideas, we have created a circulation system that all users can understand immediately upon entering the building and as they circulate through its immense footprint.

Staging is erected beneath the ceiling of the ramps for workers to restore the skylights and the plaster details.

© James Rudnick Photography

A defective corner piece of the cornice is removed and replaced with new plaster that matches the original design.

© James Rudnick Photography

A worker installs a new metal frame to match the original entrance at the corner of 42nd Street and Vanderbilt Avenue.

© James Rudnick Photography

A worker cuts the floor with a jack-hammer to open the east Oyster Bar ramp.

© James Rudnick Photography

A web of scaffolding fills the Oyster Bar ramp, providing access to all levels of the 90-foot-high space.

© James Rudnick Photography

Behind all the visual elements that have been restored there exists a greatly enhanced infrastructure, a state-of-the-art utility system that sustains Grand Central. The major improvement to this facility has been the installation of a heating, ventilation, air-conditioning system that cools the Terminal during the hot and humid summer months without bringing air in directly from the street. Above the constellations of the Main Concourse ceiling is a complex configuration of ducts that carry air from the system down inside the walls and columns to new but historically designed grille openings about twenty feet above the floor. This creates a circulation of cooled and filtered air within the building that keeps the Terminal's air fresh and the building's fabric free of destructive pollutants from the outside. During the colder seasons, the expansive space is kept warm by continuously circulating steam-heated fresh air within a more energy-efficent building where many air leaks have now been sealed. This flow creates a pressurized space that most efficiently maintains the comfortable temperature.

The fire protection system was completely overhauled and enhanced with detectors, sprinklers, and extensive exhaust systems. The rosettes on the east and west sides of the Main Concourse were once used to draw air from the interior, but they also brought grime to the ceiling and upper walls. This system is now used only in a fire emergency for smoke evacuation, and the everyday airflow is brought from the concourse by the ducts located inside the large columns on each side of the Main Concourse. Other emergency ventilation systems are located close to the platforms where fires are most likely to originate. A computerized system

Eight stories below the Main Concourse, the rotary converters, operated by Engineer of Power Jim Frawley, provide direct electrical current to the railroad lines.
Courtesy of MTA/Metro-North Collection, Frank English photographer

is designed to keep the air above a minimal breathing level so people will be able to exit the Terminal safely in the midst of a fire.

The electrical service at Grand Central is quite sophisticated. A new 13.2 kV high-voltage distribution network, which includes four feeder loops, was installed around the terminal. The system is similar to what one might find in a small village or town. Major substations are connected into high-voltage loops to serve the various facilities throughout the terminal. The primary incoming utility switch gear that connects to the loops consists of two independent Madison Avenue services from Con Edison, one from 46th Street and the other from 47th Street. Con Edison has said that these services, with all their safeties and fail-safe features, are probably the most complex of any in their service territory.

The emergency generators that are tied into the high-voltage loops are

located in two different places. The existing one is located in the Madison Avenue yards. The new generator, which Goldman Copeland Associates, Consulting Engineers designed, is located underneath Park Avenue at 48th Street. The architects worked closely with the engineers to design an enclosure to disguise the exhaust stacks, which rise in the middle of the median on Park Avenue. The entire, complex utility system of airflow, cooling, heating, and power is monitored and controlled by a computer, keeping each energy source at its most efficient output and minimizing waste.

Our early years of surveying the tunnels for all mechanical, electrical, and plumbing services at Grand Central were challenging. The team had to contend with the sometimes dangerous people who lived in these underground spaces. In addition to people being angry at our invading spaces that to many were their home, there were major potentially hazardous leaks from the old high-pressure steam pipes. In the end, the old piping was pared back and the tunnels cleaned up.

Many of our older buildings have had some of their original features hidden over time. At the east end of the Main Concourse, behind the former Chemical Bank facade, an old baggage sign was uncovered when the preparatory demolition for the east stair began. Near this location, crews unearthed the entrance to the former Grand Central Theater, formerly one of the smallest commercial theaters of its day. Hidden for many years behind the decor of a retail store that had replaced it, the entrance also revealed a dramatic and ornamental terra-cotta capital of a rather robust woman. Now this small but important piece of Grand Central's decorative art history is incorporated into the wine store occupying its location.

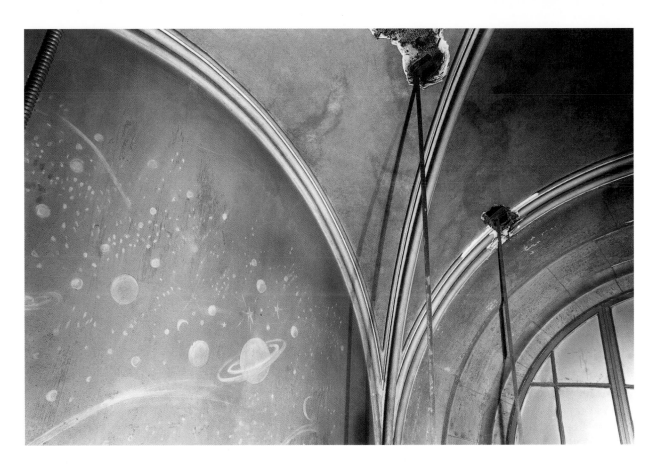

The lobby of the Grand Central Theater boasted a ceiling mural of another galaxy. Hidden behind acoustic tiles for many years, it is now restored as part of the ceiling of a wine store.

© James Rudnick Photography

The ghosts of old signage leave their markings on the Caen stone interior of Grand Central.

© James Rudnick Photography

Behind the walls of the information booth on the Main Concourse, this steamship brochure rack was uncovered. It reveals how at one time all forms of transportation were linked together for the convenience of passengers.

© James Rudnick Photography

A view along the catwalk in the attic above the sky ceiling. The ducts for the new air-conditioning system are visible crossing over the catwalk.
© James Rudnick Photography

The original sign for the baggage-check counter was exposed during the construction of the east stair.
© James Rudnick Photography

Approximately eight stories beneath the midtown streets, this stairway, surrounded by untouched Manhattan bedrock, leads to the lowest level of Grand Central.
© James Rudnick Photography

During the restoration of the information booth below the famed golden clock, a turn-of-the-century steamboat brochure rack was discovered, a testament to the fact that, at an earlier time, different modes of transportation shared information for the convenience of all travelers. The large circular information booth of glass, marble, and brass has a hidden spiral staircase connecting to the booth on the lower level so that personnel can move between the two levels.

Acorns and oak leaves, part of the Vanderbilts' coat of arms, are decoratively carved throughout the building, especially around the elevator banks and staircases in the four towers at the Terminal's corners. They are as discreet as Ninas in a Hirschfeld drawing and as difficult to find.

When several of the field architects for the restoration were asked if they had seen any ghosts during the restoration, they replied yes but of a different kind. The "ghosts" are old signage on walls throughout the Terminal that, when removed, leave a polish under the lettering. These ghosts have provided us with clues as to different aspects of the building throughout history.

In the early 1920s John W. Campbell, president of the Credit Clearing House and a major New York Central stockholder, leased from the New York Central Railroad the southwest corner space of the Terminal, just off the Main Concourse and Hall D. He created a home for himself by transforming a space twenty feet high, almost sixty feet long, and twenty-five feet wide into an eclectic mix of medieval, Romanesque, and Renaissance styles with decoratively painted walls and ceilings, a baronial fireplace, large leaded windows, and an open gallery complete with an organ. Although always described as his apartment it was primarily Campbell's office.

Like everything else in the Terminal the apartment had deteriorated by the time that the Metro-North police claimed the space as their Grand Central Police Station. Criminals were temporarily detained in what was Campbell's wine cellar, and firearms were stowed in his curio cabinet. Christopher Gray of the *New York Times* reported that when Campbell's niece Elsie Fater broke her wrist in the Terminal she asked the Metro-North police to take her to her uncle's former office, but they refused. She, along with the rest of New York, can now see this famed space again, being used for yet another purpose. As part of the Terminal's retail revitalization, the restoration of this space with its decorative features, carved woodwork, and painted walls has become home to a wine bar with a literary theme, something as extravagant and plush today as Campbell's office was in its time.

As the new stair climbs to the revived East Balcony and balances the concourse, the Oyster Bar ramp once again lifts your eyes to the heavens as you descend to the lower level. Escalators continuously roll and passages give clear and direct access. The blue and gold of the sky ceiling shine forth while the soft palette of the marble floors and Caen stone walls reclaim their elegant wonder. Brass, bronze, and gold leaf glisten in the light that pervades it all. Grand Central Terminal, an architectural vision of people moving through a space of grandeur, has been reborn.

Off the southwest corner of the Main Concourse, John W. Campbell used this space as his office for three decades. Fifty-eight feet long and twenty feet high, this Romanesque style room has been one of the best-kept secrets of Grand Central.

Avery Architectural and Fine Arts Library, Columbia University in the City of New York

A recent view of Campbell's apartment, before it was converted into a wine bar.

© James Rudnick Photography

Feb. 22. 1941

Price 15 cents

THE

NEW YORKER

CHAPTER TEN

GRAND CENTRAL AS A BAZAAR

The up-to-date station resembles a bazaar, as much as anything, in view of the thousand and one accessories people now find agreeable and necessary to have at hand when traveling.

—WHITNEY WARREN, CHIEF ARCHITECT OF GRAND CENTRAL,
NEW YORK TIMES, FEBRUARY 9, 1913

A great mix of retail stores, restaurants, and other services has always been part of the scene at Grand Central. Retail revitalization is a key element to the economic success of the restoration. Just as we had uncovered drawings to support the construction of the east stair or the reopening of the Oyster Bar ramps, we uncovered eighty years of history that spoke of Grand Central as home to rail and to retail, side by side. In 1913 there were already 69,135 square feet of retail and restaurant services. By 1930 94,531 square feet were devoted to a wide variety of businesses. Haberdashery, stationery, books, apparel, cigars, flowers, luggage, theater tickets, and pharmacies were all to be found together with a selection of newsstands, shoeshine stands, restaurants, coffeehouses, and soda fountains. To make sure that Grand Central's offerings would not be compared with just any big-city railroad station, the Terminal added its own unique blend of attractions.

Billed by its owners as "the only art gallery in the world located in a railroad station," Grand Central Art Galleries opened for business in 1923. It occupied 15,000 square feet of space above the Waiting Room on the sixth floor (currently the railroad's control room) and was an instant success. (Grand Central has a total of seven floors.) Five hundred people a day, 300,000 in its first three years, visited, saw, and purchased works of art by such artists of renown as John Singer Sargent, David Chester French, and Elliot Dangerfield. Buyers included society figures Otto Kahn, Mrs. W. K. Vanderbilt, and Helen Frick. A contemporary account described the gallery's location in a railroad station as being "psychologically" correct; "there is nothing like travel to stimulate the gland of expenditure." The gallery in later years became successful enough to open another branch on 5th Avenue at 57th Street.

A **1941** *New Yorker* **cover depicts the scene at the Oyster Bar. This particular crowd has stopped for a cup of the famous oyster stew before riding the train to the ski slopes.**

Cover drawing by Alain © 1941 The New Yorker Magazine, Inc.

If having its own art gallery were not distinction enough, in 1924 the seventh floor of the east wing (currently the railroad's training center) was converted into the Grand Central Art School. A 7,000 square foot space became six large teaching studios with newly installed skylights to provide the required north-facing natural light. The prospectus of the new school listed one course that seemed particularly at home in this Beaux Arts architecture: "Dynamic Symmetry," taught by Julian Bowes.

The growth continued into the 1930s. Even through the Depression, the Terminal flourished with commercial activity. In 1937 the Grand Central Theater opened on the east side of the Main Concourse level (currently the location of the new escalators), with 242 seats and an inglenook with easy chairs plus room for standees. It offered an hour of distraction for those who had just missed the 5:42 to Greenwich and needed to kill time before boarding the 6:48. A program of newsreels, cartoons, and shorts offered "a partial solution of the leisure time and cultural problems of the thousands of commuters and visitors using the Terminal daily," as the theater's opening publicity put it. The management even installed a large, illuminated clock beside the screen so that patrons would not miss their next train.

Carey's Barber Shop on the lower level opened around 1928 and quickly became renowned among New York's movers and shakers as the place to hear the juiciest political gossip while getting the best shave. James P. Carey had twelve other businesses in the Terminal, including two barbershops, a men's haberdashery, parcel rooms, and an agency offering chauffeur-driven Cadillac rental cars, all bearing his name.

The Oyster Bar, opened three weeks after the Terminal opened in 1913, was a classic example of a railroad station's restaurant of the highest standard. In its vast subterranean kitchen, it also prepared and cooked much of the food served aboard the long-distance trains departing from above. The Oyster Bar was known as a place that was both elegant and hearty, with one of the most crowded lunch counters in New York.

All these attractions and services brought to the Terminal not only travelers but also people who worked or lived in close proximity. By the late 1920s this population even had its own local newspaper, the *Grand Central Zone Tab*, which labeled its readers the Zoners. An issue in December 1928 carried a piece about what Zoners did on a rainy day's lunch hour, with the headline "Terminal Popular Lounging Place. On a Rainy Day; Corridors and Shops in Grand Central Packed with Those Who Fear to Brave Wet Weather."

These wonderful services began to disappear as rail travel declined in the post–World War II years. Intrusions both visual and audible assaulted the senses of Grand Central's faithful daily users. Before the Kodak sign, there were commercial displays featuring the Westclock, the Merrill Lynch Booth, and the rotating Chrysler auto display. In the autumn of 1949 the most heavy-handed attempt to introduce a new public address system began, which from 7:00 A.M. to midnight broadcast canned music, weather reports, and twenty-five commercials each hour for cigarettes, flashlights, batteries, watches, automobiles, restaurants, chewing gum, and antifreeze. Operated by the Terminal Broadcasting Company, it enraged Grand Central's users. Their anger was not assuaged by the pronouncement that they would still have to get train and track information from the old sources of the information booth and the track gates. A spokesperson for the railroad explained this omission by saying "we don't need train

A 1913 plan of the Main Concourse level shows the many services and shops occupying the spaces around the Concourse.

© Beyer Blinder Belle Architects & Planners

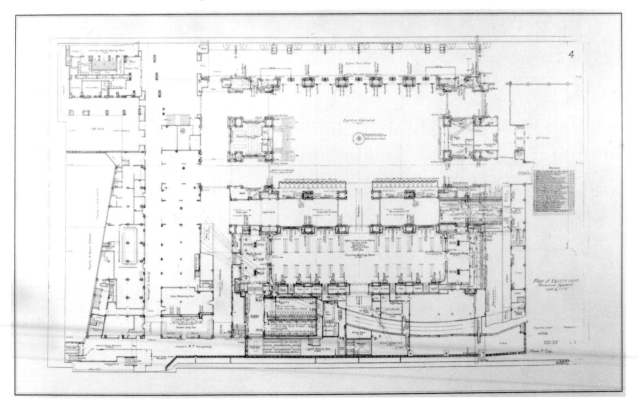

announcements here, the Grand Central system of the same train from the same track every day doesn't require train announcements." By late December the Public Service Commission had held a hearing at which many white-collar executives poured forth quiet but literate invective against this invasion of their privacy. Harold Ross, editor of *The New Yorker* and a regular commuter, brought his own brand of sarcastic humor to the cause by introducing himself to the commission as "the editor of an adult comic book." By January of 1950 the experiment that would have brought in less than $90,000 a year in income was abandoned.

As a result of falling railroad income and commercial exploitation, Grand Central became a venue for mundane retail tenants whose services and store designs were dissonant to the original bazaar concept. Tenant guidelines to keep merchandise and storefronts aligned with the Terminal's original overall intent did not exist. Lamp-heated french fries and radiating neon signs began to energize a trend that strongly conflicted with the classic theme. The railroad was unable to attract a quality of services that the grand space deserved. Offerings of the past like Carey's stylish haberdashery, fashionable jewelers, the theater, or the art gallery were replaced by fast-food counters. Any space that could offer quick and easy rent was transformed to do so, at times in a desperate manner that showed no understanding of the original role for the Terminal's retail development. A bank replaced the welcoming, much-used, baggage claim desk beneath the east balcony. The steel and glass Merrill Lynch stock booth sat in the middle of heavily trafficked circulation paths in the Main Concourse. The lofty ramp to Vanderbilt Avenue and 42nd Street was compromised in order to provide space for the Kitty Kelly shoe store, and later it became an outlet for Federal Express. Grand Central receded into a forum of limited services and stores that rashly forecast higher profits

Spend An Hour With Auer
AT THE
AUER HEALTH STUDIOS
New York's Most Exclusive Establishment
OF
Exercises,   Medicine Ball,   Baths,
Electric Cabinets,   Massage.
Expert European Masseurs and Masseuses.

PATRONIZED BY
New York's Most Prominent Business Men
and Society Women.

FOR THE RELIEF OF
Obesity,   Thinness,   Stomach Trouble,
Constipation,
OR
An Overworked and Rundown Condition.

MOST CONVENIENTLY LOCATED
IN THE
NEW GRAND CENTRAL TERMINAL.
(42d Street, at Vanderbilt Avenue)
SUITE 4217-4123

Here Two Entirely Separate Departments,
Each Complete in Itself,
Are Maintained for Men and Women.

Call and see me personally   or,   Telephone Murray Hill 1067

Located on an upper floor of Grand Central, the Auer Health Studio offered therapeutic relief for overworked New Yorkers in the 1920s and 1930s.
Courtesy of MTA/Metro-North Collection

Grand Central Theatre, a 242-seat movie theater with a cocktail lounge, opened in 1937 and showed newsreels, shorts, and cartoons for three decades.
Courtesy of MTA/Metro-North Collection

than was feasible. People no longer ventured into the Terminal for reasons other than necessary commutation. The once posh bazaar fell to the entropy of the "quick buck."

This downward spiral accelerated during the 1960s and 1970s. What had been a wonderful range and variety of services was replaced by an endless succession of doughnut, bagel, and bric-a-brac stores.

An important part of the restoration mission was to restore the original style and mix of services, not only for travelers but also for all New Yorkers who lived in, worked in, or passed through Grand Central's neighborhood. The Terminal's retail services were once more going to be decidedly for and of New York. A merchandising master plan was developed as a worthy companion to the restoration master plan. The challenge was to develop a plan that set high standards, built upon the uniqueness of the location, and created a balanced mix of tenants that together would become a popular destination for many different users.

Intense discussions with many participants were led by Susan Fine, Jean Giordano, and Williams Jackson Ewing Inc. We knew that we didn't want to suburbanize our urban center. We wanted to attract the best of New York's diverse merchants. Many sorties were made in search of the perfect soup shop (Mike's Take Away), the best cheesecake (Juniors), the freshest flowers (Flowers on Lexington), a fashion store with a true New York flare (Kenneth Cole), an international newsstand (Eastern News), and a good old-fashioned bookstore (Posman Books)—all with the right New York touch.

In fitting the many component parts into one cohesive plan, the danger was making commitments to an individual merchant's needs that would permanently compromise Grand Central's historic fabric and circulation patterns—probably its two most distinctive features. For example, on the lower level the former suburban concourse has become the dining concourse with 28 food merchants and seating for 650 diners. The rationale for this component of the merchandising plan was that, unlike other major spaces in the Terminal that were kept active throughout the day by people constantly passing through them, the lower concourse ceased to be active between morning and evening rush hours. Hence the concept of making this space a dining destination would give

people a reason to visit it during the daytime and evening hours. But it would be a challenge to develop a specific plan to achieve this new use while keeping the traditional circulation paths to the tracks clear and retaining the concourse's significant historic features such as the unused ticket windows.

The solution was to locate the food merchants in areas that were not directly in the path of either traditional or new circulation elements and then create an overall layout to which every merchant would be able to conform. Two tenant zones were created on each side of the historic Ticket Window wall. The zone behind the wall is for kitchens and food preparation, using the former ticket windows as pass-throughs to the front zone, which is used for food display and customer service. There are no actual sealed storefronts; simple, steel-framed arches give each merchant a sign location and an identity. Should there be the need at some future time to restore the railroad ticketing function to the lower level (perhaps because the Long Island Railroad will bring some of their trains into Grand Central as their east-side access point), the current merchandising layout could be reverted back to assume a railroad function. Reversibility such as this is always part of good restoration planning, and our merchandising plan was developed with this in mind. Nobody can be sure that decisions made today will be sustained indefinitely; a good plan needs to propose modifications that do not destroy the basic character of the building.

Just as the original Terminal had possessed an overall approach emphasizing clear and direct paths of circulation, our revitalization plan worked to

The remodeled Lexington Passage is lined with small shops that have floor-to-ceiling bay windows, adding floor space to small boutiques and a feeling of greater spaciousness to a low-ceilinged arcade.

© Peter Aaron/Esto

emulate that. This foundation gave us the opportunity to lay out the retail spaces in a clear thematic manner providing the merchants and their clientele with the best shopping bazaar and avoiding the ubiquitous identity of chain merchants so prevalent in typical malls. Given that the same rules that governed any change in the Terminal applied here, storefronts for these shops had to be consistent with the historic fabric. John H. Beyer and Margaret Kittinger, Beyer Blinder Belle's director of interiors, worked closely with Williams Jackson Ewing to develop a design that gave merchants a modern floor-to-ceiling storefront with an enframement that used the historic colors and materials of the original retail spaces.

An early effort had focused on trying to find the right combination of restaurant, cafe, and bar to occupy the vast space that had been the original Waiting Room. Influenced by the experience of a series of temporary events, Christmas and Easter fairs, art exhibits, concerts, and performance events, a different approach was ultimately taken for this space. The best combination turned out to be a mix of revolving uses similar to the experimental, temporary

A model depicts the original suburban Lower Concourse redesigned as a Dining Concourse. A selection of the city's finest eateries, a circular juice bar, and an arched-roof dining room now share this space with continuing train activity. Original benches from the historic Waiting Room are incorporated into the new layout.
© The Rockwell Group, Beyer Blinder Belle Architects & Planners/ Jock Pottle/Esto

events that had filled the former Waiting Room (renamed Vanderbilt Hall) throughout the first two years after its restoration. The MTA, Metro-North, and GCTVenture, to their credit, wanted to maintain a level of art within the Terminal, and Vanderbilt Hall (the former Waiting Room) is that venue. Sarah Horowitz, director of programming and special events for the GCTVenture, developed a program and a place that will be a forum for artists, craftspeople, unique retailers, and performers to continue the experimental program on a permanent basis.

The restaurants and bars originally planned for Vanderbilt Hall have migrated to the balcony spaces surrounding the Main Concourse. Set sixteen feet above the floor level, these balconies are the perfect location for sitting and watching the action below.

As the overall restoration construction progressed, negotiations with the tenants who would lease the 119 individual retail and restaurant spaces throughout the Terminal were also proceeding. Part of the original approvals given by the city and state landmark agencies was contingent on the team returning to review further and approve individual plans for these tenants when they would be occupying significant historic locations in the Terminal—especially the parts of the interior that were officially designated as landmark spaces. Unfortunately, in their eagerness to secure first-class tenants for these spaces, the leasing agents did not fully disclose to the tenants some of the constraints that had been imposed by the landmark agencies when the original plans were approved. Leasing is at best an imprecise and creative activity, and its practitioners sometimes tend to "simplify realities." The balcony restaurants' approval was subject to 20 percent of the total space remaining accessible to the general public. The purpose of this condition was to ensure that everyone, not just patrons of the restaurants, had an opportunity to view the glories of the restored Concourse from the vantage

One of the two dining rooms fashioned on the profile of a Pullman dining car with large photo murals located where windows would have been located.

© Peter Aaron/Esto

point of the balconies surrounding it. To their credit, both Joan K. Davidson, as New York State's commissioner of historic preservation, and Jennifer E. Raab, as chair of New York City's Landmarks Preservation Commission, expressed strong support of this objective. However, despite their efforts, public access to the balconies is considerably less than originally intended.

The first balcony restaurateur to submit plans was Peter Glazier, who proposed that a steak house and bar be installed on portions of the west and north balconies. David Rockwell, his architect, was an immensely successful and talented designer of New York restaurants who was also working on the designs for the Dining Concourse on the lower level. By the time the details of the lease were made known to us it was too late to alter the reality that the deal cut with Glazier did not require that 20 percent of his space be publicly accessible. Since his space on the west balcony included one of the two original Vanderbilt Avenue entrances that we had hoped to reopen as public entrances, it was particularly disturbing that the proposed layout did not include this public feature. Working closely with Rockwell on the designs for the Dining Concourse, we did not feel the need to second-guess him. However, the morning after reassuring the Landmarks Commission that the steak-house-in-a-railroad-station was compatible with the overall plans and receiving their approval, we were greatly surprised by the announcement on November 25, 1997, in the *New York Times* Metro section in an article by Florence Fabricant, "Coming Soon: Michael Jordan's Steak House." This signaled to the architects, the Landmarks Preservation Commission, and the civic watchdogs like the Municipal Art Society and the New York Landmarks Conservancy that Grand Central was still prone to excessive commercialism and that we would need to keep our guard up in the future.

Fortunately, the two restaurants occupying the other prominent balcony spaces offered design concepts much more respectful of the Terminal. On the East Balcony, now approached from the new grand stairs, Matthew Kenney's restaurant Metrazur has a Mediterranean theme and a classic, restrained design by Calvin Tsao that is very respectful of the restored architecture. On the Vanderbilt Avenue balcony, Arrigo Cipriani of Harry's Bar fame has created Cipriani Dolce, a classic European railway station bar and restaurant in a stylish and traditional manner.

At a time when physical changes to the Terminal seemed to be appearing everywhere and every day, we were jolted by change of a different kind. One June morning, reminiscent of the one in which Paul Goldberger wrote about Grand Central basking in light, a call came from Mark Nusbaum in our field office. "Have you seen the Godzilla banner on the East Balcony?" *Godzilla*, the movie intended to be the blockbuster of the summer of 1998, had opened a few weeks earlier to lukewarm reviews. To boost its sagging business, a 115-foot-long, almost totally black vinyl banner with a 30-foot depiction of Godzilla's claw on it had been erected across the arched windows that we had "liberated" from the Kodak sign during the early days of the restoration campaign. The effect was to completely obliterate the morning sunshine that commuters had grown to enjoy

Taste

FOR well over a decade now, the owners of Grand Central have been turning that once noble building into a tawdry indoor Times Square, ablaze with advertisements. Every foot of wall and floor that could be made to pay off pays off; only the vaulted ceiling of the main concourse fails to yield a profit, and we've no doubt that some advertising JD will eventually find a way to make those twinkling constellations spell out your favorite smoke, like a constellation should. The bastardizing of the terminal began, as we recall it, with mechanized ads; then came canned commercials, broadcasts over a loudspeaker system (we had a little to do with putting a stop to *that*); and now a brand-new gimmick has been introduced and given a two week trial run—something called living billboards.

We went over to Grand Central last week to observe the first of these billboards in operation and to check up on some of the other indignities to which the poor old beauty is being subjected. From the look of things, the reasoning of the owners must go about like this: "What we'd really like to do is pull the concourse down, because all the empty air it holds ought to be producing revenue. Still, the building is much admired by students of architecture, lovers of New York, and other cranks, who will raise holy hell if we lay a hand on it. Holy hell is bad public relations. Therefore, the smart thing to do is to combine making money with vulgarizing the terminal to the point where those who admired it most will be the ones most eager to have it done away with." If anything like that logic lies back of what is currently going on at Grand Central, we congratulate the owners on their success. No shooting galleries yet, no gypsy fortune-tellers, but nearly everything else is to be found there, including cars (on a revolving turntable), cameras, hi-fi, woodworking tools, office furniture, and a young man who urges passersby to purchase waterfront lots in Port Charlotte, Florida, for ten dollars down and ten dollars a month over eighty-eight and a half months.

The living billboard consists of a large, framed sign that serves as a sort of stage; it rests on the flat roof above the bank of New York Central ticket windows, at the south side of the concourse, and is linked by means of a concealed passageway to a dressing room on the balcony. Three young women hired by the dress-manufacturing concern of Andrew Arkin, Inc., model dresses three times daily—at 9 A.M., noon, and 5 P.M. We went over to the terminal in time to catch the noon show, which proved to be some minutes late; a hundred or so people had gathered in front of the ticket windows and were waiting patiently for the girls to come on. The crowd was predominantly male, and we heard one of the few women present complain to her companion that the men were there not to buy dresses but to ogle. "Turning Grand Central into a free burlesque show!" she said. "Isn't it disgusting?" Her companion, a male, made no reply.

We asked one of the ticket agents on duty under the living billboard whether he'd seen the show. "Not yet," he said. "I can hear them flopping around up there, though, getting ready." We put an ear to his window and, sure enough, heard the tip-tapping of high heels from somewhere above. "That mob out there makes it look as if we're selling a lot of tickets," the agent said. "Maybe it will be good for business, at that."

Having watched the girls model four dresses apiece, in the fast time of twenty five minutes forty seconds, and in a manner not at all like that of a burlesque show, we joined Charles McArthur Jr., of the McArthur Advertising Corporation, at the rear of the crowd, and put a couple of pertinent questions to him. The McArthur Corporation, which has charge of most of the advertising in the terminal, is particularly pleased with itself for having devised the living billboard. "Living billboards have a great future, provided they're not done to death," said Mr. McArthur, with the air of a man who has made a mot and knows it. "Over four hundred thousand people walk through Grand Central every day. A lot of them are dress buyers, and will stop and take a look at Arkin dresses. Arkin is paying us two thousand a week for the billboard; that includes the cost of the girls. All signs have to be in good taste. Our keynote is dignity. Kodak alone pays a hundred and twenty five thousand dollars a year, for the east balcony. The cheapest space we sell in the main concourse goes for sixteen thousand seven hundred dollars a year, including the cost of the signs. All a matter of size and location." McArthur's eyes drifted up toward Orion, and we made our excuses and fled.

By Brendan Gill

as a welcome start to their day. A few hours after Nusbaum's call the architectural team stood in the Main Concourse with sinking hearts. It didn't matter that MTA spokespersons were giving public statements that this was only a temporary event and that it was not their intention to go back to the old days when the Terminal was a merchandising venue filled with signs and kiosks. The signal that was sent seemed to confirm the ad agency spokesperson's statement that "it was a great opportunity to reach a target market during a very important month, probably the highest profile ad location in New York," and seemed a more honest assessment of things to come. People wanted to know why this and why now. Editorials in the *New York Times* and letters to the editor reflected the public's outrage.

This incident served as a reminder that the act of restoring a building to its original state is only half the battle; the other half is to guard against its denigration throughout its future existence. With that in mind, it is worth recalling

During the 1950s, a living billboard of young women model vacation clothes above the ticket offices in the Main Concourse.

Corbis/Bettmann ©

a piece that originally appeared in *The New Yorker* in 1958 written by Brendan Gill, who, although not then as bitten by the preservation bug as in later years, still managed to get to the heart of the matter.

Forty years after Gill wrote this piece, do we need to be concerned about our restored building being turned over to Mr. McArthur's successors? For the moment Godzilla's departure has happened as quickly as his unwelcome arrival. But no doubt lurking out there is an enterprising young account executive with no taste but lots of ambition, who will latch on to the Terminal's reinvented fame as the perfect locale for his or her client's ailing or booming product and make a persuasive pitch to MTA executives just as they are grappling with the gap in their next five-year financial plan.

In this way perhaps nothing will have changed except that our daily use of the restored Terminal will have instilled in us all, including ambitious account executives and harried public officials, a greater determination to protect Grand Central from the excesses of the past. And we hope that the "reversibility" of our plan will give the Terminal the flexibility it will need to continue in its new life without again having to deal with insensitive and inappropriate commercialization.

CHAPTER ELEVEN

INTO THE TWENTY-FIRST CENTURY

Grand Central Terminal's newly restored state brings to mind many questions. Whatever made anyone think that this monument should be demolished? Why did the railroad allow the great space above the Oyster Bar ramps to be used for utilitarian ticket offices? Was the original constellation ceiling really this blue? Were the Caen stone walls this creamy? Did the chandeliers sparkle the same way when they were first turned on?

These and other questions are prompted by a degree of disbelief that the restoration of this important building is now complete, making it ready for a new century of service. Having failed to save so many landmarks, it isn't surprising that an observer's first reaction is often "Am I dreaming? Pinch me." But there is no disputing the factual evidence of the photographs that follow. They document reality not fantasy, concrete accomplishments not pipe dreams.

Observing this phenomenon from the architect's point of view, the wonder is that Whitney Warren's original building and our restoration have been accepted by today's users as being seamlessly one and the same. Certainly the terminal's newly reconstructed circulation system with generous open passages leading directly from its core to the surrounding city is at the heart of people's comfort. The quality of the building's materials, their colors, and their textures all confirm that, despite its monumental scale, the Terminal's primary function is to welcome each and every traveler—a function that it can now perform as it was meant to.

Whatever functioning changes are in store for Grand Central Terminal over the next hundred years, there is every reason to be confident that it will exist and perform admirably.

At dusk, the Terminal's facade, though surrounded now by skyscrapers, signals its presence as a gateway to the city. What it lacks in sheer mass it makes up for in classical Beaux Arts design and superb limestone and granite materials.

© Peter Aaron/Esto

The Park Avenue viaduct defines the
approach to the building. It forms a
giant plinth upon which the entire
Terminal appears to sit with storefronts and entrances set into its 42nd
Street level like jewels set into a
crown.

© Peter Aaron/Esto

A new entrance on Lexington Avenue at 43rd Street has one of the cast iron eagles which originally decorated the 1899 Grand Central Station.

© David Sundberg/Esto

The main entrances to the Terminal at Vanderbilt Avenue and 42nd Street, Vanderbilt Avenue and 44th Street, and Park Avenue and 42nd Street all offer the visitor a sheltering welcome under canopies of different shapes and materials. A scalloped glass canopy curving around a corner, a straight angled canopy running parallel to the 42nd Street sidewalk, and a Guastavino tiled ceiling in a deeply recessed and well-sheltered taxi stand bring people into Grand Central.

© Peter Aaron/Esto

The Main Concourse is entered at each of its four corners by passing through graceful, low, arched openings. The contrast of each opening with the monumentally scaled Main Concourse adds to one's sense of having arrived at the gateway to the city. The concourse measures 200 feet long by 120 feet wide by 125 feet high. The two symmetrically placed staircases, one original and the other newly installed, sit between the four entry points on the long east-west axis of the concourse. Daylight streams through the three arched windows at either end as well as through the smaller lunette windows, set like eyebrows into the edges of the sky ceiling.

© Peter Aaron/Esto

Ticket windows and new train indicator boards are on the south side, and train platforms are on the north side; information is dispensed at the center of the space. This timeless arrangement for a train station still works superbly through its directness and clarity.

© Peter Aaron/Esto

For the first time in the Terminal's history the view to the right is identical with that to the left, as the new east stair (left) complements its eighty-five-year-old companion west stair (right). Symmetry and clear circulation are finally in balance.

© Peter Aaron/Esto

Upon entering the Terminal, newly restored passageways lead visitors toward the Main Concourse. Direct sight lines and a high level of visibility give a strong sense of security to all users. The interior lighting is enhanced with additional light fixtures that are historic, accurate, and produce the light levels expected in today's public buildings.

© Peter Aaron/Esto

Above: As if lying down and gazing up at the heavens, the viewer can observe the constellation almost in its entirety, as Paul Helleu conceived it. But the formal composition of the stars and zodiac signs is actually reversed and depicted from a viewpoint in the heavens looking down toward Earth. Astrological realism was not the objective of either the architect or the artist; they created a formal design complementing the proportions of the classical architecture of the Main Concourse and dramatizing the limitless sense of space.

Left: The cerulean blue of the sky ceiling contrasts dramatically with the white of the ornamental plaster-work that frames both the lunette windows and the arched end walls of the concourse. To the left where the gold-leaf band meets the orna-mental plasterwork, a small dark patch of unrestored paint and plas-ter shows the ceiling's condition before the restoration.

© Peter Aaron/Esto

Orion brandishes his staff to keep spirits at bay.

© Peter Aaron/Esto

The two staircases, one old and one
new, vary in some of their details.
The original staircase was designed
long before contemporary laws were
enacted to protect the disabled and
physically impaired. The solid
balustrade of the original west stair
terminates two steps above the floor
to accentuate the feeling of flowing
onto the concourse. A brass handrail
was added to provide the required
support. Also, as part of the west
stair's design, the marble stair wall
ends in an ornately carved scroll
emblazoned with the signature of the
Vanderbilt family: oak leaves and
acorn decorations. The new staircase
on the east side has a stair wall that
extends beyond the last step to conform with handicap regulations without the addition of a protruding
brass rail. The modern detailing of
the stair wall and the balustrades
reflects a simpler contemporary
design. Great care was taken to match
the Bottocino and Tennessee marbles
of the original stair through numerous field visits to the stone quarries
in Tuscany and Tennessee.

© Peter Aaron/Esto

The tricorn-shaped light hangs over each ticket window and is lit up when service is available. The opalescent glass lamps are hung from nickel and brass ornamental brackets; some of the brackets are of original historic fabric and some are newly designed and fabricated to match.

© Peter Aaron/ Esto

Viewed from the west end of the Main Concourse, the line of ticket windows resembles the linear form of a train's curvaceous observation car. The polished and etched brass grilles that surround the ticket clerks were made to match the details discovered in historic photographs of the original ticket windows. New luggage racks have been installed at a more convenient height for commuter luggage than the original position, which accommodated the large bags used by long-distance travelers.

© Peter Aaron/Esto

Modern technology has brought new elements to the Terminal. The new indicator boards give train arrival and departure information more efficiently, and the new bronze grilles immediately above, through which tempered air cools the interior, are carefully designed and scaled to fit with the historic details of the Main Concourse.

© Peter Aaron/Esto

One of the most noticeable changes to the Terminal since its restoration is the increased presence of light throughout the building. Sometimes the sun penetrates deep into the building's interior through previously impenetrable, dirt-encased windows; sometimes the light from newly restored chandeliers bounces off mirrored windows. Everywhere, the light colors of the cleaned stone, plaster, and marble interior surfaces contribute to the building's glow from within.

© Peter Aaron/Esto

With five glittering chandeliers above, restored marble and Caen stone walls on either side, and a new balustrade on the bridge crossing over from Vanderbilt Hall (formerly the Waiting Room) to the Main Concourse, the ramps have become a new space for New Yorkers to experience. A glimpse of the Main Concourse sky ceiling between the stone piers gives ramp users a visual reference back to the heart of the Terminal.

© Peter Aaron/Esto

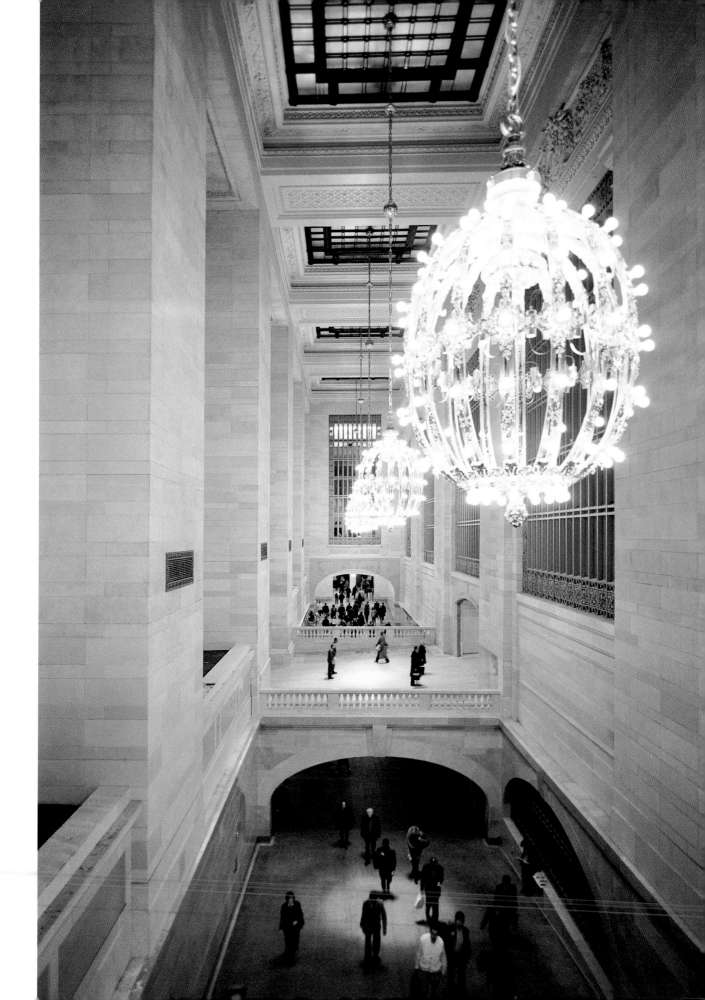

The bar of Michael Jordan's Steak
House sits beneath one of the great
arched windows in the Terminal's
west facade with a classic view of the
Beaux Arts architecture. The windows serve as corridors linking
offices on the Terminal's north and
south upper levels.

© Peter Aaron/Esto

To allow daylight to penetrate into the Main Concourse from the east and west, Whitney Warren designed these corridors as tubes of glass and steel through which sunlight could pass. Before the advent of air conditioning, the windows were designed as an operable ventilation system with a rack-and-pinion mechanism to pivot open both inner and outer leaves of windows. With the installation of a new air-cooling system, the windows will remain closed, keeping the air of the Main Concourse comfortable and clean.

© Peter Aaron/Esto

The North Balcony is divided into two by escalators leading up from the Main Concourse to the MetLife Building. In the foreground a stair with its original historic balustrade has been preserved and now leads down to a storage level for a balcony restaurant.

© Peter Aaron/Esto

Opposite: The Graybar Passage has been restored and refurbished with new retail services by the Graybar Building owners and the MTA. The mural is by Edward Trumbull, who is also the artist of the ceiling murals of the Chrysler Building lobby. The light-colored passageway with plaster and travertine finishes blends well with Grand Central's overall style.

© Peter Aaron/Esto

Above: The opening of the Oyster Bar ramps—as the ramps leading down to the original lower concourse have been popularly called for many years—has been received with astonishment. Now the walk down is no longer a dangerous descent into the unavoidable unknown.

© Peter Aaron/Esto

Throughout the Terminal, intricate details of ornamental metalwork, plasterwork, light fixtures, and staircases give human scale to the monumentality of the Beaux-Arts architecture.

© Peter Aaron/Esto

Just off the Main Concourse on the west side of the Terminal, a new Station Masters Office has been created with a customer service desk, a supervised waiting room, and public bathrooms. As part of the Arts for Transit program, a mural by Roberto Juarez decorates the room. Passengers wait for their trains on the historic benches that were located in the original Waiting Room.

© Peter Aaron/Esto

STATION
MASTERS
OFFICE

GRAND CENTRAL TERMINAL

CUSTOMER
WAITING
ROOM

A new experience at Grand Central is
to stand on the landing of the east
stair looking toward the west stair
and the Vanderbilt Avenue entrance
from a viewpoint elevated above the
concourse floor.

© Peter Aaron/Esto

EPILOGUE

It took ten years to build Grand Central Terminal and ten years to restore it; both efforts, in their own way, symbolize their respective eras. It is estimated that to build Grand Central today would cost approximately $1.7 billion rather than the $80 million price tag in 1913—assuming there was will enough to take on such a task. Despite the complexity of subterranean construction and the lack of modern engineering technologies in the early twentieth century, which certainly prolonged construction by today's standards, the speed of the design and public approval process probably could never be matched again. It was and still remains an example of city building at a gargantuan scale, at a break-neck pace.

About a century ago, the shape and nature of Grand Central passed through three different built forms: the original Depot, the Station, and the Terminal. Each essentially wiped out its predecessor. All came into existence because our society believed that new was better than old, that the future had little or nothing to learn from the past.

This philosophy, which guided our urban growth and the development of most twentieth-century architecture, continued unchallenged until the 1960s. As a result, we lost a great deal of our historic fabric and the cultural memories that went with it—Grand Central's sister, Penn Station, included. Thanks to a pioneering band of preservationists, who were generally considered freaks on the fringe by most of their fellow citizens, Grand Central's third embodiment, the 1913 Grand Central Terminal, survived the trend to become the focus of our decade-long restoration. On the threshold of the millennium, to have this great building ready for another century of use is both a symbolic and a factual achievement of great significance. It reflects a more mature society that is not driven to destroy its past in order to meet its future needs.

Consensus is yet to be reached on what the future transportation needs of this metropolitan region will be, and what will be Grand Central's specific role in the overall scheme. The newly restored Grand Central is not only a noble gateway to the city once more, but also an essential component in the struggle to deal with tomorrow's transit needs. Thanks to the vision of its original builders, its capacity has still not been reached, either in the number of trains accommodated by its tracks or the population flowing daily through its terminals. Given the increase in vehicles attempting to squeeze into midtown Manhattan each day, we may yet learn to maximize the use of Grand Central to improve the quality of our daily life.

The MTA is moving ahead with the planning necessary to eventually bring Long Island Rail Road trains into the east side of Manhattan by using some of the tracks on Grand Central's lower level. Next should come the consideration of making the Terminal the point of departure and arrival for the city's airports via high-speed light rail trains. On a local scale, with the rebirth of the theater district and the emergence of parkland along the Hudson River, this would be the time to build a 42nd Street crosstown trolley, a unique crosstown route that was part of the original concept for Grand Central.

Because Grand Central is no longer a tired, shabby monument that people are afraid to enter, its influence on our traveling habits could become far-ranging. Grand Central has a purpose beyond its role as a commuter railroad station and once more reaffirms its role as a city within a city. The five-day-a-week commuters can now bring their families into the city by train on weekends—rather than having to drive—to go to a museum, see a show, or watch a ball game via Metro-North and a welcoming Grand Central.

In the fall of 1998, on the occasion of the rededication of the building, Paul Goldberger, architectural critic of *The New Yorker*, wrote these words at the completion of his critique, "The Sky Line: Now Arriving," originally published in *The New Yorker*:

> Grand Central teaches us that monumental architecture can transcend issues of refinement and enrich the minutiae of daily life. The building, with its swarming crowds, is an oasis of calm, a serene eye in the midst of the swirling city. If you doubt this, look at how many people are not rushing through the Main Concourse but stopping to contemplate it. And it is somehow inherent in the nature of the space that, however large the crowds, people direct themselves around each other, intuitively; the concourse is not a hectic passageway of jostling throngs but an immense dance floor.
>
> Now that Grand Central no longer functions as a place for long-distance arrivals and departures, it is more like a town square. Its clarity and its serenity, as well as its majesty, belong to everyone, and not, as they once did, primarily to those coming to board the Twentieth Century Limited. A transcendent experience is there for the taking, even if you're only walking through.

Grand Central's ability to adapt to the needs of the thousands upon thousands of people passing through in a manner of singular calmness embodies truly great architecture, and it stands as a daily reminder that the future depends upon our willingness to confront and address our urban problems with both a sensitivity to the past and a concern for our future.

APPENDIX: PLANS

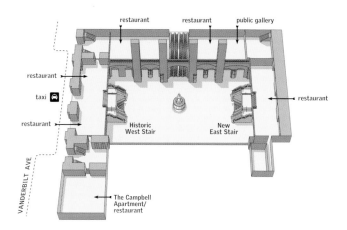

restaurant   restaurant   public gallery

restaurant

taxi

restaurant

Historic
West Stair

New
East Stair

restaurant

VANDERBILT AVE

The Campbell
Apartment/
restaurant

Balcony Level

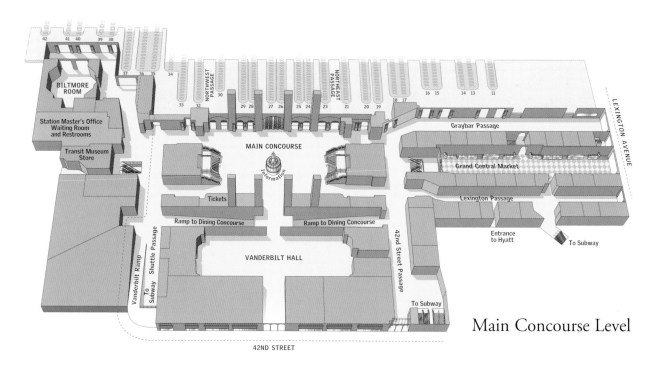

42   41   40   39   38

BILTMORE
ROOM

37   36   35   34

NORTHWEST PASSAGE

30

NORTHEAST PASSAGE

Station Master's Office
Waiting Room
and Restrooms

33   32   29 28   27 26   25 24   23   21   20   19   18 17   16 15   14 13   11

Transit Museum
Store

MAIN CONCOURSE

Information

Graybar Passage

Grand Central Market

LEXINGTON AVENUE

Tickets

Lexington Passage

Ramp to Dining Concourse   Ramp to Dining Concourse

Entrance
to Hyatt   To Subway

Vanderbilt Ramp

Shuttle Passage

To Subway

VANDERBILT HALL

42nd Street Passage

To Subway

Main Concourse Level

42ND STREET

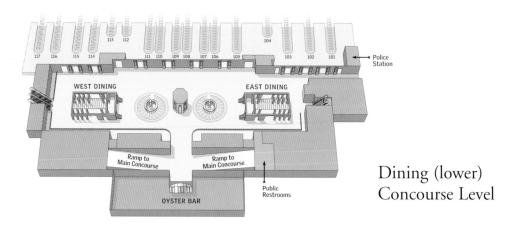

113   112   104

117 116   115 114   111 110 109 108 107 106 105   103 102 101

Police
Station

WEST DINING   EAST DINING

Ramp to
Main Concourse   Ramp to
Main Concourse

Public
Restrooms

OYSTER BAR

Dining (lower)
Concourse Level

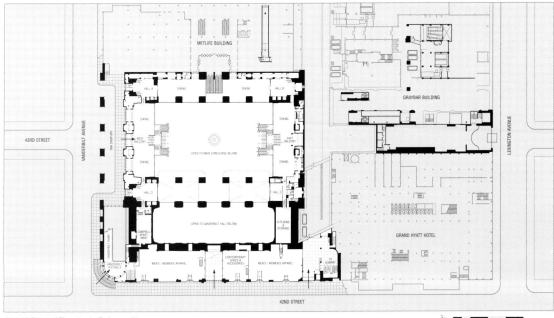

Grand Central Terminal: Balcony Plan

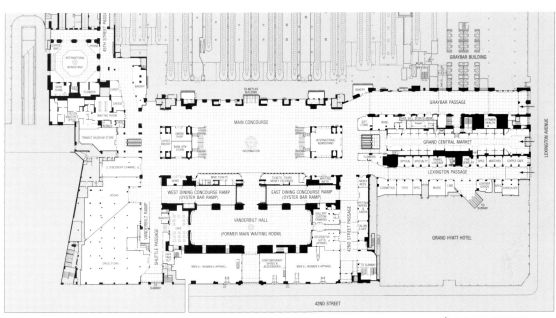

Grand Central Terminal: Main Concourse Plan

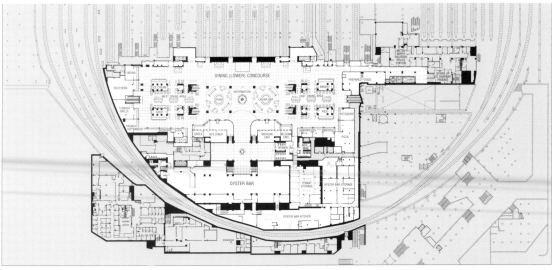

Grand Central Terminal: Dining (Lower) Concourse Plan

BIBLIOGRAPHY

"Adventurous Performers in Unexpected Place." *New York Times*, October 9, 1987: C1, C36.

"A Glory of the Metropolis." *New York Times*, February 2, 1913: II 16: 2.

"A Victory for Preservation U.S. Supreme Court Decision in Grand Central Case." *Heritage Newsletter* Vol. 6, No. 3 (September 1978): 1–4.

"Airplane Bremen is Suspended in Central Terminal." *Grand Central Zone Tab*, May 24, 1929.

"All Day in Grand Central Station." *New York Times*, February 24, 1924: IV 3.

Alleman, Richard. *The Movie Lover's Guide to New York*. New York: Perennial Library, 1988.

"All of New York's Tumult Jammed into a Terminal." *New York Times*, December 28, 1991: L23.

"America's Trysting Place Number One." *New York Times*, August 2, 1936: 6.

"An Impressive Battery of Legal Talent Joins the Battle to Save Grand Central Terminal from Demolition." *New York Times*, July 30, 1972: 18.

Anthony, Carl Sferrazza. *As We Remember Her*. New York: HarperCollins Publishers, 1997.

"Architects Beat Plan for Grand Central Bowling." *Architectural Forum* Vol. 114, No. 2 (February 1961): 9.

"Architects Hit Plans for Grand Central Bowling." *Architectural Forum* Vol. 114, No. 1 (January 1961): 9.

"Architect Wins His 500,000 Appeal." *New York Times*, February 10, 1920: 7: 1.

"Artists in Grand Central." *New York Times*, August 21, 1924: 10: 7.

"Ban of Grand Central Office Tower Is Upheld by Supreme Court 6 to 3." *New York Times*, June 27, 1978: A1.

Bartlett, John. *Familiar Quotations*. Boston: Little Brown and Company, 1875.

Beals, Kathie. "Can Grand Central Outlast Time?" *Daily Times*, Mamaroneck, New York, October 4, 1975: A8.

Beebe, Lucius. *20th Century*. Berkeley, Cal.: Howell-North Books, 1962.

Bernard, Walter. "The World's Greatest Railway Terminal." *Scientific American*, June 17, 1911: 594–95, 609–10.

Bickel, Alexander M. *The Supreme Court and the Idea of Progress*. New York: Harper & Row Publishers, 1970.

"Big Doings at the Depot [Theatre at Grand Central]." *New York Times*, May 9, 1937: XI 3: 5.

Birmingham, Frederic A. "Grand Central Station." *Holiday* 44, August 6, 1968: 26–29, 75–76.

Bissell, Elaine. "Radio Serial Chronicled Terminal's Story." *Daily Times*, Mamaroneck, New York, October 4, 1975: A8.

Blake, Peter. "In Defense of an Outrage." *New York*, August 12, 1968: 50–52.

"Born Again." *On Track* (April 1996): 1, 4–5.

"Bowling Over Grand Central." editorial, *New York Times*, January 10, 1961: 46.

"Broadcasting in Railroad Stations." *New York Times*, September 8, 1949: 28: 5.

Breuer, Marcel. "An Architect of the Inevitable." *Village Voice*, July 25, 1968: 3.

Bruere, Robert W. "The Gates of New York." *Outlook*, April 27, 1907: 927–42.

"Buys Grand Central Terminal for $1,200." *New York Times*, March 29, 1921: 5: 2.

"Buy Your Masterpieces Between Trains." *New York Times*, March 18, 1923: IV 4.

Calhoun, Charles W., ed. *The Gilded Age, Essays on the Origins of Modern America*. Delaware: Scholarly Resources, 1996.

"Can the Grand Central Concourse Be Saved?" *Architectural Forum* Vol. 5 (November 1954): 134–39.

Carley, Clyde. "This Is Grand Central." *Railway Progress*, Vol. 2 (May 1957): 4–9.

"Celebrities Ride the Rails to Save Grand Central." *New York Times*, April 17, 1978: D9.

"Central Terminal Opening on Sunday." *New York Times*, January 29, 1913: 13: 1.

"Children in Rush to Summer Camps." *New York Times*, June 28, 1943: 24: 5.

"Christmas Songs." *New York Times*, December 24, 1943: 12: 3.

"City Folks Crowd New Grand Central." *New York Times*, February 3, 1913: 3: 6.

"City within a City." *New York Times*, September 28, 1924: II 1: 4.

Collins, Nancy. "Riding the Rails for Grand Central." *Washington Post*, April 17, 1978: B1.

Condit, Carl W. *The Port of New York: A History of the Rail and Terminal System from the Grand Central Electrification to the Present*, 2 vols., Chicago: University of Chicago Press, 1980.

Cook, Richard J., Sr. *The Twentieth Century Limited 1938–1967*. Lynchburg, Va.: TLC Publishing, 1993.

"Court Rules Against Landmark: Grand Central Case Decided." *Preservation News*, Volume 15, No. 3 (March 1975): 1: 9.

"Design of 'Grand Central City' Accepted." *Progressive Architecture* (March 1959): 157.

Drexler, Arthur, ed. *The Architecture of the Ecole des Beaux Arts*. New York: Museum of Modern Art, 1977.

Droege, John A. *Passenger Terminals and Trains*. Reprint. Milwaukee: Kalmbach Publishing Company, 1969.

Dunlap, David W. "Grand Central, Reborn as a Mall." *New York Times*, August 2, 1968: 33, 36.

Dunlap, David W. "Fixing Leaking Roof at Grand Central." *New York Times*, August 24, 1987: B3.

Edwards, H. R. "Colossus of Roads." *Railroad Stories*, Vol. 20 (November 1936): 4–23.

"The Enlargement of Grand Central Station, New York." *Engineering News*, January 6, 1898: 12–14, 126–28.

"Erecting the Grand Central Terminal." *Engineering Record*, August 24, 1912: 222–23.

"Expert Says Only 'Tetched' Suffer from Terminal 'Ads'." *New York Times*, December 23, 1949: B1.

Fabricant, Florence. "Coming Soon: Michael Jordan's Steak House" *New York Times* November 25, 1997.

"Farewell to Penn Station." *New York Times*, October 30, 1963: 38.

"First Step in Grand Central's Grand Plan." *Crain's New York Business*, May 29, 1989: 2.

Fischer, Edward G., with Amos, Wayne. "Everything Happens at Grand Central Station." *Collier's*, Vol. 133, March 5, 1954: 86–89.

Fitch, James Marston, and Waite, Diana S. *Grand Central Terminal and Rockefeller Center; A Historic-critical Estimate of Their Significance*. New York State Parks and Recreation, Division for Historic Preservation, 1974.

"Flowers for Poor at Grand Central." *New York Times*, June 11, 1922: II 7: 8.

"Flowers for the Flowerless." *New York Times*, June 11, 1922: II 6: 4.

"Foreigners at Grand Central." *New York Times*, October 9, 1913: 12: 5.

"43,000,000 in 1927 Use Grand Central." *New York Times*, December 14, 1927: 40: 1.

Franz, Robert. "Haskell on Grand Central." *Architectural Forum* Vol. 131, No. 1 (July–August 1969): 12, 16.

The Gateway to a Continent. New York: New York Central System, c. 1938.

Gilbert, Frank. "The Grand Central Case." *Preservation News* Vol. 162, No. 2 (February 1976): 12.

Gilmartin, Gregory F. *Shaping the City, New York and the Municipal Art Society*. New York: Clarkson Potter, 1995.

"A Glory of a Metropolis." *New York Times*, February 2, 1913: II 16: 2.

Goldberger, Paul. "City's Naming of Grand Central as a Landmark Voided by Court." *New York Times*, January 22, 1975: 1: 6.

Goldberger, Paul. "Grand Central Reinstated as a Landmark by Court." *New York Times*, December 17, 1975: 33: 1.

Goldberger, Paul. "Grand Central Basks in a Burst of Morning Light." *New York Times*, June 30, 1990: 227.

Goldberger, Paul. "The Skyline: Now Arriving." *The New Yorker*, September 28, 1998: 92–94.

Goldman, Philip H. "Grand Central." Letter to the editor, *Architectural Forum* Vol. 102, No. 1 (January 1955): 78.

"Goodbye, No. 1." *On Track* (May 1996): 5.

"Grand Central Appeal Wins: New York Landmarks Law Upheld."

Preservation News (February 1976): 1–7.

"The Grand Central Art Galleries." *New York Times*, March 21, 1923: 16: 5.

"Grand Central Bauhaus." *Progressive Architecture* (April 1968): 52–53.

"Grand Central City." *Architectural Forum* Vol. 129, No. 1 (July–August 1968): 72–73.

"Grand Central Depot Signal System." *Scientific American*, December 25, 1875: 399–402.

"Grand Central Development Seen as Great Civic Center." *Engineering News-Record*, September 9, 1920: 496–504.

"Grand Central Gets Vanderbilt Statue." *New York Times*, November 29, 1928: 40: 6.

"Grand Central Installs Chime." *New York Times*, August 23, 1940: II: 2.

"Grand Central Railway Station; New York Central and Hudson River Railroad, New York." *Engineering*, May 30, 1913: 725–27.

"Grand Central Reborn." *New York Times*, October 2, 1998: A28.

"The Grand Central Riot: Yippies Meet the Man." *Village Voice*, March 28, 1968: 13, 14.

"Grand Central Shops: Customers on the Run." *New York Times*, October 28, 1979: 1, 9.

"Grand Central's Outdoor Concourse." *Architectural Forum* Vol. 100, No. 2 (February 1954): 116–19.

"The Grand Central Terminal." *Fortune* (February 1931): 97–99.

"Grand Central Terminal Opening on Sunday." *New York Times*, January 29, 1913: 13: 1.

"Grand Central Terminal Used by 64,719,574 in '45." *New York Times*, January 25, 1946: 35: 2.

"Grand Central Wins Court Victory." *Progressive Architecture* (February 1976): 32.

"Grand Central Zone Boasts Many Connected Buildings." *New York Times*, September 14, 1930: VIII 11: 2.

"Grand Guignol." *New York Times*, April 2, 1990: 25.

"Gratitude for Beauty." *Grand Central Zone Tab*, February 1, 1929.

Gratz, Roberta B. "City May Drop Landmark Status for Grand Central Terminal." *New York Post*, November 8, 1974.

Gratz, Roberta B. "Court Weighs Grand Central Status." *New York Post*, October 22, 1975: 16.

Gratz, Roberta B. "Mayor in Production to Fight Departure of Grand Central." *New York Post*, April 21, 1977: 17.

Gray, Christopher. "The End of the Line for Grand Central's Big Picture." *New York Times*, June 18, 1989: 8.

Gray, Christopher. "In a Forgotten Corner, a Curious Office of the 20's." *New York Times,* "Streetscapes," October 11, 1998: 11: 7.

Gray, Christopher. "The 23-Story, Beaux-Arts 1913 Tower That Wasn't." *New York Times*, "Streetscapes" (real estate section): 7.

"The Great Railway Terminal of the Future." *New York Times*, February 9, 1913: VI 9: 1.

"Gropius-Belluschi-Roth Design for Grand Central City." *Architectural Record* Vol. 125, No. 3 (March 1959): 10.

Haskell, Douglas. "The Lost New York of the Pan American Airways Building." *Architectural Forum* Vol. 119, No. 5 (November 1963): 106–11.

Haskell, Douglas. "Visionless Enterprise." *Architectural Forum* Vol. 113, No. 4 (October 1960): 87.

Haskell, Douglas. "Futurism With Its Covers On." *Architecture Review* Vol. 157, No. 939 (May 1975): 300–304.

Helprin, Mark. *Winter's Tale.* San Diego: Harcourt Brace and Company, 1983.

Henry, Diane. "Jackie Onassis Fights for Cause." *New York Times*, January 31, 1975: 37.

Hill, O'Harrow, and Weinberg. "Grand Central." Letters to the editor, *Architectural Forum* Vol. 102, No. 6 (June 1955): 76, 80, 84, 88.

Hiss, Tony. *The Experience of Place.* New York: Alfred A. Knopf, 1990.

"Holdup Attempt, Shots and Chase Stir Grand Central." *New York Times*, September 11, 1920: 1: 6.

"Holiday Music at Grand Central." *New York Times*, November 18, 1940: 8: 6.

"Homeless Respond to Aid at Terminal." *New York Times*, August 12, 1989: 2.

Horsley, Carter B. "Air War: Grand Central Terminal Transfer Deal Would Raise Tower Almost as Tall as Chrysler." *New York Post*, April 20, 1989: 39: 1.

"The Hotel Commodore, New York." *Architecture Review* (August 1919): 69–75, pl. 40–48.

"Hot on the Trail for Celebrities." *New York Times*, January 29, 1939: VII 15: 1.

Howells, William Dean. *A Hazard of New Fortunes.* New York: Harper & Brothers, New American Library, reprint, 1965.

Hungerford, Edward. "The Greatest Railroad Terminal in the World." *Outlook*, December 28, 1912: 900–911.

Huxtable, Ada Louise. "Architecture: How to Kill a City." *New York Times*, May 5, 1963: II: 15.

Huxtable, Ada Louise. "Slab City Marches On." *New York Times*, March 1968: 22, 1.

Huxtable, Ada Louise. "Architecture: Grotesque Astride a Palace." *New York Times*, June 1968: 37.

Huxtable, Ada Louise. "Grand Central: Its Heart Belongs to Dada." *New York Times*, June 23, 1968: 10, 4.

Huxtable, Ada Louise. "The Stakes Are High for All in Grand Central Battle." *New York Times*, April 11, 1969: 28.

Huxtable, Ada Louise. "Why Did We Lose Grand Central as a Landmark?" *New York Times*, January 31, 1975: 26–27.

Huxtable, Ada Louise. "How Great Buildings Shape a City's Soul." *New York Times*, October 19, 1975: II: 32.

Huxtable, Ada Louise. "Grand Central at a Crossroads." *New York Times*, January 29, 1978: II: 25, 28.

Huxtable, Ada Louise. "A 'Landmark' Decision on Landmarks." *New York Times*, July 9, 1978: II: 21, 24.

Huxtable, Ada Louise. "On the Right Track." *New York Times*, November 28, 1994 (op. ed.).

"An Impressive Battery of Legal Talent Joins the Battle to Save Grand Central Terminal From Demolition." *New York Times*, July 30, 1972: 18: 1.

"Improvement of the Grand Central Station, New York." *Railroad Gazette*, June 23, 1899: 447–49.

Inception and Creation of the Grand Central Terminal. New York: privately printed for Allen Stem and Alfred Fellheimer, 1913.

Inglis, William. "New York's New Gateway." *Harper's* Vol. 47, No. 2, February 1, 1913: 13, 20.

"Interpreters at Grand Central." *New York Times*, October 15, 1913: 10: 5.

"Is Grand Central Terminal 'Outmoded'? Owners Consider Replacement Schemes." *Architectural Record* Vol. 116, No. 5 (November 1954): 20.

"Jackie Onassis Fights for Cause." *New York Times*, January 31, 1975.

Jackson, Kenneth T., ed. *The Encyclopedia of New York City.* New Haven: Yale University Press, 1995.

Johnson, Weldon James. *Black Manhattan*. New York: Da Capo Press, reprint, 1991.

Josephson, Matthew. *The Robber Barons*. New York: Harcourt Brace & Company, 1962.

"J. P. Carey Will Open Seventh Barber Shop in Middle of July." *Grand Central Zone Tab*, May 10, 1929.

"Jumbo Atop Grand Central." *New York Times*, June 20, 1968: 44.

Kauffman, Edgar, Jr. "The Biggest Office Building Yet . . . Worse Luck." *Harper's* Vol. 220 (May 1960): 64–70.

Klein, Aaron E. *The History of the New York Central System*. New York: Bonanza Books, 1985.

Knight, Carleston, III. "New York City Landmarks Law Upheld." *Preservation News* (February 1976): 1, 7.

"Landmark Preservation—A Survey." *Art and the Law* Vol. 2, No. 4 (April–May 1976): 2–4.

Landmarks Preservation Commission. Grand Central Terminal Designation Report (LP–0266). New York: City of New York, August 2, 1967.

Landmarks Preservation Commission. Grand Central Terminal Interior Designation Report (LP–1099). New York: City of New York, September 23, 1980.

Lynes, Russell. "Stacked-Up." *Harper's* Vol. 237, No. 1421 (October 1968): 38–42.

MacVeigh, Sue. *Grand Central Murder*. Boston: Houghton Mifflin Company, 1939.

"Manning to Unveil Model of Cathedral Today in Grand Central Terminal for Exhibition." *New York Times*, December 10, 1931: 27: 3.

Marshall, David. *Grand Central*. New York: Whittlesey House, McGraw-Hill Book Company, 1946.

Meeks, Carroll L. V. *The Railroad Station: An Architectural History*. New York: Dover Publications, 1995 (original publication by Yale University Press, New Haven, 1956).

"Mendel's Is Out of Grand Central." *New York Times*, February 1, 1919: 9: 3.

Middleton, William D. "The Grandest Terminal of Them All." *Trains* Vol. 35 (May 1975): 22–35.

Middleton, William D. *Grand Central, The World's Greatest Railway Terminal*. San Marino, Cal.: Golden West Books, 1977.

Middleton, William D. "Grand Central Terminal Restored." *Railway Gazette International* (December 1998).

"Model of St. John's Unveiled by Bishop." *New York Times*, December 11, 1931: 20: 3.

"Monumental Gateway to a City." *Scientific American*, December 7, 1912: 473, 484–87, 499–501.

"More Jobs for Women." *New York Times*, August 19, 1942: 22: 5.

Moscow, Warren. "Protests Cause End Tonight of Grand Central Broadcasts." *New York Times*, January 2, 1950: 1: 2.

Muschamp, Herbert. "Grand Central as a Hearth in the Heart of the City." *New York Times*, February 4, 1996: 27.

Muschamp, Herbert. "Restoration Liberates Grand Vistas, and Ideas." *New York Times*, October 2, 1998: B6.

"Music at Grand Central." *New York Times*, March 24, 1937: 27: 2.

Myers, Debs. "Grand Central Terminal." *Holiday* 13 (March 1953): 64–68, 70, 72, 73, 131, 133–34.

Nevins, Deborah, et al. *Grand Central Terminal, City within a City*. New York: The Municipal Art Society, 1982.

"New Art Gallery Opens to Throngs." *New York Times*, March 22, 1923: 18: 8.

"New 5,000,000 Hotel for Grand Central." *New York Times*, April 22, 1916: 7: 6.

"The New Grand Central Station in New York." *House and Garden* (February 1905): 63–65.

"New Home for Art to Cost $100,000." *New York Times*, March 11, 1923: II: 7, 5.

"A New School of Art." *New York Times*, June 17, 1924: 8: 1.

"New York Central Says It May Quit City, Close Terminal." *New York Times*, July 3, 1958: 1: 5.

"New York Central to Furnish Music." *New York Times*, November 20, 1939: 16: 3.

"New York City's Landmarks Gives Grand Central a Reprieve." *Architectural Record* Vol. 146, No. 4 (October 1969): 37.

"New York Grand Central Railway-Station." *Construction & Engineering Review*, December 27, 1912: 781–86.

"New York's New Gateway." *Harper's* Vol. 47, No. 2 (February 1, 1913): 13, 20.

"Only Art Gallery in a Railroad Station Is a Paying Institution." *Grand Central Zone Tab*, September 28, 1928.

"The Opening of a Great Railroad Terminal." *Engineering Record*, February 8, 1913: 235, 258–59.

"Opening of the New Grand Central Terminal, New York City." *Engineering Record*, February 8, 1913: 142.

"The Pan Am Building: A Behemoth Is Born." *Progressive Architecture* Vol. 44, No. 4 (April 1963): 61–62.

Parissien, Steven. *Pennsylvania Station*. New York: Phaidon Press Limited, 1996.

Parissien, Steven. *Station to Station*. London: Phaidon Press Limited, 1997.

Patterson, Jerry E. *The Vanderbilts*. New York: Harry N. Abrams, 1989.

"Plan New Heaven for Grand Central: Leaky Roof Has Filled Present Sky with Tramp Comets and a Mildewed Way." *New York Times*, April 11, 1924: 16: 1.

"Plan to Update Grand Central Station." Promotional Publication. *Architectural Forum* Vol. 101, No. 4 (October 1954): 41.

"Policing the Grand Central." *New York Times*, February 15, 1931: V 17: 2.

"Progress on the Grand Central Terminal." *Railway Age Gazette* Vol. 53 (November 22, 1912): 981–86.

"Protests Stir the P.S.C. to Ponder Halt to Grand Central Broadcasts." *New York Times*, December 13, 1949: 1: 2.

"The Railroad Commissioners on the Tunnel Collision." *Railroad Gazette*, February 7, 1902.

Rau, Deborah Fulton. Historic Structures Report. Printed privately by Beyer Blinder Belle Architects & Planners LLP, New York, 1992.

Rau, Deborah Fulton. *The Development of the Sky Ceiling in the Evolution of Grand Central Terminal, 1903–1994*. Privately printed, © Deborah Fulton Rau, 1994.

"Remodeling the Grand Central Station, New York." *Engineering Record*, June 17, 1899: 56–58.

"Revamped Terminal Puttin' on the Ritz: Grand Central Rededicated Today." *New York Times*, October 1, 1998: B6.

"Revised Grand Central Station, (the) New York City." *Railroad Gazette*, February 19, 1887: 126–28.

The Revitalization of Grand Central Terminal. Published privately by Metropolitan Transportation Authority, GCT Venture and Beyer Blinder Belle, New York, 1994.

Richards, Jeffrey, and MacKenzie. *The Railway Station: A Serial History*. New York: Oxford University Press, 1986.

Roth, R. "The Forces that Shaped Park Avenue." *Perspecta* (1963): 97–102.

Sachs, Susan. "From Gritty Depot, a Glittery Destination." *New York Times*, October 2, 1998: B1–B6.

Salinger, J. D. *Catcher in the Rye*. New York: Little, Brown & Company, 1951.

Saltzman, Steven, and Senft, Bret. "Grand Central Terminal." *Metropolis* (September 1991): 17–24.

"Save the Concourse." Letters to the editor, *Architectural Forum* Vol. 102, No. 2 (February 1955): 116–19.

"Saving a Station." *Time*, July 10, 1978: 26.

"Scenic Views Shown on Terminal Screen." *New York Times*, April 10, 1947: 19: 1.

Scheiner, Seth M. *Negro Mecca*. New York: New York University Press, 1965.

Schmertz, Mildred. "The Problem of Pan Am." *Architectural Record* Vol. 133, No. 5 (May 1963): 151–58.

Schneider, Walter S. "The Hotel Biltmore." *Architectural Record* Vol. 35 (March 1914): 222–45.

Scully, Vincent. "The Death of the Street." *Perspecta* 8 (1963): 91–96.

"Some of the Fundamental Principles of Air Rights." *Railway Age*, October 22, 1927: 757–59.

"Space Under Concourse to Be Used for Stores." *Grand Central Zone Tab*, September 21, 1928.

"State Scenic Exhibit to Rise in Terminal." *New York Times*, August 4, 1935: II 6: 7.

"Stationmaster's Life: Central, But Not Grand." *New York Times*, October 16, 1998: B2.

Stern, Robert; Gilmartin, Gregory; and Massengale, John. *New York 1900*. New York: Rizzoli International Publications, 1983.

Stern, Robert; Gilmartin, Gregory; and Mellins, Thomas. *New York 1930*. New York: Rizzoli International Publications, 1987.

Stern, Robert; Mellins, Thomas; and Fishman, David. *New York 1960*. New York: The Monacelli Press, 1995.

Stetson, Damon. "World's Loftiest Tower May Rise on Site of Grand Central Terminal." *New York Times*, September 8, 1954: 36, 1.

"Strange Finds on Trains: More than 15,000 Articles Turned in Annually at Grand Central." *New York Times*, September 19, 1920: VII: 2, 7.

Stringer, Lee. *Grand Central Winter*. New York: Seven Stories Press, 1998.

"Support Grows for Saving Grand Central Concourse." *Architectural Forum* Vol. 101, No. 6 (December 1954): 37.

Tafel, Edgar. *About Wright*. New York: John Wiley & Sons, 1995.

"Talk of the Town: Click, Click." *The New Yorker*, October 16, 1948: 25–26.

"Talk of the Town: Grand Central." *The New Yorker*, February 10, 1975: 27–29.

"Talk of the Town: Kitty Kelly Airborne." *The New Yorker*, October 17, 1959: 33–34.

"Talk of the Town: Notes and Comment." *The New Yorker*, June 29, 1968: 23.

"Talk of the Town: Renaissance." *The New Yorker*, November 18, 1974: 47–48.

"Talk of the Town: Rigid." *The New Yorker*, June 9, 1945: 16–17.

"Talk of the Town: Taste." *The New Yorker*, November 15, 1958: 47–48.

"Taxing Away the Railroads." *New York Times*, April 27, 1955: 30: 3.

"Ten Killed, Scores Hurt in Explosion: Pintsch Gas Blast Brings Death and Ruin at Grand Central Station." *New York Times*, December 20, 1910: 1: 7.

"Terminal Popular Lounging Place on a Rainy Day." *Grand Central Zone Tab*, December 7, 1928.

"Theatre for Commuters." *New York Times*, September 9, 1936: 49: 8.

"38,260,143 Passengers Used Terminal in Year." *New York Times*, February 14, 1940: 25: 2.

Thompson, Hugh. "The Greatest Railroad Terminal in the World." *Munsey's Magazine* (April 11): 27–40.

Tolchin, Martin. "Demolition Starts at Penn Station; Architects Picket." *New York Times*, October 29, 1963: 1: 24.

Toth, Jennifer. *The Mole People*. Chicago: Chicago Review Press, 1993.

"Tower Over Grand Central Barred as Court Upholds Landmarks Law." *New York Times*, June 27, 1978: 1, B2.

Trager, James. *Park Avenue, Street of Dreams*. New York: Atheneum, Macmillan Publishing Company, 1990.

"Travelers Hear Chorals." *New York Times*, April 12, 1936: 3: 4.

"[Christmas] Trees in Grand Central." *New York Times*, December 19, 1929: 26: 8.

Twain, Mark, and Warner, Charles Dudley. *The Gilded Age, A Tale of Today*. New York: Meridian/The Penguin Group, 1994.

"218.9($) Million Loss Is Listed by Pennsy." *New York Times*, March 6, 1976: 31, 38.

"Veins of Marble." *On Track* (February 1996): 1–2.

"Viewing the Kaleidoscope of New York." *New York Times*, December 20, 1936: VIII 12: 3.

Wagner, Walter F., Jr. "The Wrong Criticism, in the Wrong Place, at the Wrong Times." Editorial, *Architectural Record* Vol. 144, No. 3 (September 1968): 9–10.

"Waldorf-Astoria." *Architecture and Building* (December 1963): 147–53.

Waldron, Webb. "Fortune Was Found in the Search for Good Will." *Century Magazine* (November 1926): 41–49.

The Warren and Wetmore Collection, Avery Library, Columbia University, New York.

Weaver, Warren, Jr. "Tower Over Grand Central Barred as Court Upholds Landmarks Law." *New York Times*, June 27, 1978: 1: 2.

West, Cornel. *Keeping Faith, Philosophy and Race in America*. New York/London: Routledge, 1993.

Wharton, Edith. *House of Mirth*. Reprint. New York: Bantam Books, 1983.

Whitaker, Rogers E. M., and Hiss, Tony. *All Aboard with E. M. Frimbo.* New York: Kodansha International, 1997.

Wilgus, William J. "The Grand Central Terminal in Perspective." *Transactions of the American Society of Civil Engineers Paper* (1941): 992–1051.

The William J. Wilgus Collection, The New York Public Library, New York.

Williams, Frank. "Grand Central City." *Architectural Forum* Vol. 128, No. 1 (January–February 1968): 48–55.

Williams, Jesse Lynch. "The Gates of the City." *Century Magazine* (August 1907): 487–500.

Wolfe, Thomas. *You Can't Go Home Again.* New York, London: Harper & Row Publishers, London 1940.

"World's Largest Sculpture Group for New York." *New York Times,* June 14, 1914: V 8: 2.

"[A Mural Picture Shows that America is] Worthwhile Defending." *New York Times,* December 10, 1941: 24: 4.

ACKNOWLEDGMENTS

We are indebted to our editor Jim Mairs, who guided us through this, our first book together, with his patience and enthusiasm for the project. We thank him and the manuscript editor, Nancy Palmquist, along with Katy Homans who designed the book, and her associate Jacqueline Goldberg. We are grateful to our agent, Lane Zachary of Zachary Shuster, for her extraordinary encouragement and counsel. William Bickford, our researcher and writing assistant, deserves special mention.

We thank the Furthermore Foundation and Joan K. Davidson for their generous grant, which enabled us to more profusely illustrate our story; the John F. Kennedy Library and Caroline Kennedy Schlossberg for their permission to print Jacqueline Kennedy Onassis's letter to Mayor Beame, and the Municipal Art Society for access to their archives. Among the employees of the libraries, archives, and public agencies who aided us in research with their collections, we are especially indebted to Claudia Gisolfi, MAS Information Exchange; Tracy Calvan, Phyllis Cohen, Municipal Art Society; Marjorie Anders, Wayne Ehmann, Frank English, Patricia Raley, Metro-North; Fred Courtwright, Neil Hoos, W. W. Norton; H. Lansing Vail, Jr., New York Central System Historical Society; Mary Beth Betts, New-York Historical Society; Janet Parks, Dan Kany, Avery Architecture and Fine Arts Library, Columbia University; William Middleton, Allen Roberts, Railroad Enthusiasts Club; and Christopher Gray, Office of Metropolitan History.

This book would not have been possible without the people who agreed to share their personal knowledge. We owe them a debt of gratitude: Kent Barwick, Laurie Beckelman, Himan Brown, Paul Byard, Nina Gershon, Roberta Gratz, Flora Hardy, Hugh Hardy, Sarah Horowitz, Philip Johnson, Jack Kerr, Michael McLendon, Leonard W. Maglione, Dorothy Miner, Sal Monti, Frederick S. Papert, Peter Samton, Robert L. Smith, Peter Stangl, Countess Sylvia Szapary, Gladys Szapary, Adele Chatfield-Taylor, David Treasure, Alfred Vanderbilt, Jr., Margot Wellington, Margo Warnecke, and Clark Whelton. A note of thanks to Mary Jane Augustine of Baer Marks & Upham and Thomas Roberts of Beldock, Levine & Hoffman, whose guidance was invaluable. And Suzanne Farrell for the loan of her island hideaway to JB that became such a productive writing retreat.

We want to make special mention of those writers who inspired us, opened new perspectives, and challenged our own point of view. And though their work is cited in the bibliography, we wish to thank them beyond the literal debts: Carl Condit, David Dunlap, Dr. James Marston Fitch, Brendan Gill, Paul Goldberger, Tony Hiss, Ada Louise Huxtable, David Marshall, William Middleton, Herbert Muschamp, Deborah Nevins, Deborah Fulton Rau, Andy Rooney, Mildred Schmertz, Cornel West (who shared his story with MRL for the book), and Carter Wiseman.

To the firm of Beyer Blinder Belle and the partners, associate partners, associates and staff who supported our efforts; and most especially to those who bore the weight of our absence as we wrote in stressful solitude: Marilyn Marullo, Jennifer Ganley, Anne Edris, Jennie Pocock, and Richard Southwick.

The authors wish to thank their friends, families, and significant others for their patience and support.

TO ALL THOSE WHO WITH HEAD HEART AND HAND
TOILED IN THE CONSTRUCTION OF THIS MONUMENT TO
THE PUBLIC SERVICE.   THIS IS INSCRIBED

CREDITS

As is always the case in the field of historic preservation, there are many to thank who worked in the care and saving of Grand Central Terminal and its restoration. This list is just a portion of the many people it takes to keep the momentum going for ten years on a project of such magnitude.

Governor George E. Pataki
1994–present
Former Governor Mario M.
Cuomo 1982–94
Former Mayor Edward I. Koch
1978–89
Former Mayor David N. Dinkins
1990–93
Mayor Rudy W. Giuliani
1994–present

**The New York City Landmarks
Preservation Commission**
Laurie Beckelman, Chairman,
1990–94
Jennifer J. Raab, Chairman,
1994–present
Alex Herrera, Director
Preservation Department,
Emeritus
William Neeley, Jr., Deputy
Director Preservation
Department

**NYS Historic Preservation
Office**
Joan K. Davidson,
Commissioner, 1993–94
Bernadette Castro,
Commissioner,
1995–present
Winthrop Aldrich, Deputy
Commissioner for Historic
Preservation, 1993–present

**Advisory Council of Historic
Preservation**
Mary Ann Nabor

**The New York Landmarks
Conservancy**
Peg Breen
Roger Lang

Municipal Art Society
Kent Barwick
Laurie Beckelman
Doris Freedman
Jack Kerr
Jacqueline Kennedy Onassis
Frederick Papert
Whitney North Seymour, Sr.
Margot Wellington

Master Plan Consultants: 1988–94

Original Master Plan and specific aspects of the restoration: A Cooperative Venture of Beyer Blinder Belle, Harry Weese Associates and STV/Seelye Stevenson, Value and Knecht

Harry Weese Associates
Stan Allen, former President of HWA
Harry Weese, former Chairman of HWA
Karl J. Landesz
Tim Werbstein

STV/Seelye Stevenson, Value and Knecht
Dominick M. Servedio, President and Chief Executive Officer
Benjamin Bank
Marcello Belia
David L. Borger
James Chen
John F. Culhane
Kishor Doshi
Michael Friedman
Ike Goldman
Lucian Gonzalez
Richard A. Hardy
Garo Koumjian
Joseph J. Lucca
Paul A. Papay
Linda Rosenberg
Peter Ruiz
Peter Schuller
Albert L. Thompson
Greg Vachon
Alexander Varvarian
Conor Wrafter

Utilities Engineer
Goldman Copeland Associates, P.C.
Charles C. Copeland, Principal
Howard R. Holowitz, Principal
Eric Arsenicos
Colin Brennan
Benjamin Byerson III
Kismet F. Cummings
Frank List
Michael Love
Roberto Resoraro
Les Switzer
Robert Uomoleale

Electrical Engineer
GG Engineering
Geri G. Dhlopolsky

Field Survey
Taylor Architects
Adina Taylor
Roberto Velasco Architect

CADD Base
L.E. Tuckett Architect

Architectural Materials Conservation
Integrated Conservation Resources, Inc.
Glenn Boornazian, Principal

Lighting
Fisher Marantz Stone
Paul Marantz, Principal
Richard Renfro, Principal Emeritus
Barry Citrin
Sara McBarnette
Tina Periquet
Matt Toomajian

Architectural Graphics
Vignelli Associates
Massimo Vignelli, President
Lella Vignelli, Chief Executive Officer
Janice Carapellucci
David Law
Rocco Piscatello
Rebecca Rose

Acoustics/Public Address System
Shen Milsom & Wilke, Inc.
Fred Shen, Principal
Peter Berry
Linda Miller
Mark Reber

Cost Estimating
AMIS Inc.
Jay Schondorf, Principal

Historic Paint & Color Analysis
Welsh Color & Conservation
Frank S. Welsh, Principal

Code Consultant
Schirmer Engineering Corporation
John Devlin, Principal
John Deubler
Stephen Hill

Security
Schiff & Associates, Inc.
Gary Schiff, Principal
Mark Bennett
William Mckool

Traffic/Transportation
Vollmer Associates
Daniel W. Greenbaum, Partner
Chi Chan
Greg Del Rio
Mike Feeney
Thomas R. Harknett

Revitalization Project: 1994–99

GCT Venture, Inc. (a joint venture of Jones Lang LaSalle and Williams Jackson Ewing)—Program Managers & Leasing Agents

Williams Jackson Ewing, Inc.
Michael J. Ewing, Principal
W. Lehr Jackson, Principal
Roy F. Williams, Principal
S. Rae Baymiller
Michael J. Crimmins
Sunny Y. Choi
Jane A. Ehrenkranz
J. Kenneth Kauffman
Robert E. Kinsey
Jacqueline G. Klinger
R. Alexandra Kustow
James A. Lennon
William Matias
Margaret A. Meginniss
Thomas M. Murray
John W. Roane
Kathleen T. Sawin
Joseph D. Seeds

Jones Lang La Salle
William J. Chizmar, Senior Vice President
Jack J. Tenanty, Senior Vice President
Jonathan E. Bortz, Managing Director
Robert F. Works, Managing Director
Curtis C. Battles, Vice President
Andrew L. Cairns, Vice President
Cubie H. Dawson, Jr., Vice President
Deborah E. Leonard, Vice President
Mark Teare, Vice President
Stephen R. Schlegel, Eastern Region President

Daniel M. Alter
Dawn Banket
Laurie Beckelman
Flora Bourne
Christine Brownson
Damon Chapman
Molly Collins
Monica Frost
Cynthia A. Garcia
Sarah Horowitz
Jessica Hughes
Timothy B. Jackson
Cindy Juskiewicz
Paul Kastner
Kenneth L. Keenan
Miriam Martinez
Fiona Morgan
Gregg Nunziata
Daniel Quinn
Lynda M. Roca
Marcia Rubinstein
Patrick T. Shiels
Jack D. Train
Hossein Youssefi
Lloyd Zuckerberg

Revitalization Project Oversight
RWG Associates
Richard Griffiths, Principal

M/E/P Engineer
Goldman Copeland Associates, P.C.

Electrical Engineer
GG Engineering

Structural Engineers
Ysrael A. Seinuk, P.C.
Jeffrey Smilow, Vice President
Carla DaCosta
Michael Ressner
James Rzeckowski
Belinda Tello

Structural Engineers (Main Concourse)
STV/Seelye Stevenson, Value and Knecht

Structural Engineers (Retail)
Gilsanz Murray Steficek
Phil Murray, Principal

Architectural Production
Sen Architects
Robin Sen, Partner
Rashmi Sen, Partner
Suneet Jain
Eric Mullen

Architectural Materials Conservation
Integrated Conservation Resources, Inc.

Base Building Architectural Graphics
Vignelli Associates

Retail Graphic Design/Signage/Illustrators
212/Harakawa, Inc.
Ann Harakawa, Principal
Ellen Conant
Colleen Hall
Maira Kalman
Patricia Kelleher
Sheri Koetting
Laszlo Kubinyi
Lisa Mooney
Patrick Nolan
Nicole Richardson
Jared Schneidman
Steven Stankiewicz

Lighting
Fisher Marantz Stone
Paul Marantz, Principal
Richard Renfro, Principal Emeritus

Vertical Transportation
Van Deusen & Associates
John A. Van Deusen, Principal
Nicholas Lombardi
Mike Sori

Code Consultants
Schirmer Engineering Corporation

Field Support & Specifications
Federman Design + Construction
Consultants Inc.
Paula Tocci Federman, Principal
Paul Lochart
Richard Scanlon
Tom Zabriskie

Restaurant / Market Consultant
Hugh A. Boyd Architects
Hugh A. Boyd, Principal

Lower Concourse Food Court Design
Rockwell Group
David Rockwell, Principal
Edmund Bakos
Linda Dinkins
Lorraine Knapp
Erica Prichard

Tenant Mechanical Criteria
Energy Economics, Inc.
Gary M. Elovitz, Principal

Public Relations

The Kreisberg Group
Louisa Kreisberg, President
Claire Whittaker,
Senior Vice President
Peter Carzasty, Vice President
Bree Jeppson
Scott Watson

Matz Arzt & Shea
George Arzt, Principal
Clark Whelton,
Executive Vice President
Fielding Dupry,
Executive Vice President Emeritus

Miles of Media
Jamie Miles, Principal
Jennie Morgan

Renderers
Architectural Dilenator:
Portofolio, Inc.
Kevin Woest, Principal

Oliveros & Friends
Edmond S. Oliveros, Principal

Model Maker
3D Design
Leslie Murray, Principal

Photography
Esto Photographics
Peter Aaron
Jock Potell
Erica Stoller
David Sundberg

James Rudnick Photography,
James Rudnick

Contractors

Waiting Room Restoration Project
George Campbell Associates,
General Contractor
George Campbell, President
Eric Campbell

*Retail, Main Concourse and
Utilities Projects*
Lehrer McGovern Bovis, Inc.,
Construction Manager / General
Contractor
Peter Marchetto, President
Joan E. Gerner,
Senior Vice President
Joseph Monaco,
Senior Vice President
Brian E. Peters,
Senior Vice President
Steven H. Sommer,
Senior Vice President
Maury Best
John Bonavita
Frank A. Casale
Mildred Castanon
George Churchill
Sara L. Cicerone
Mary J. Costello
Philip Walter Davidson
Dawn Marie DeIure
Hugh Doherty
Richard P. Dotson
Russell R. Gilroy
Paul Jay Gingold
Sander Goldman
Joseph J. Gusera III
Phillip Hartten, Sr.
Nancy Hayes-Davis
Dean Michael Hennedy
Steven K. Holness
John S. Hyers, Sr.
Michael J. Izzo
Dean E. Jacobson
Kenneth Kaiser
Leonard Kelleher
Shari L. Krugman
Beth Leahy
Sylvia Lightbourne
Kevin Lucas
Vincent Vi Chi Luoung
Kevin A. Mangan
Richard X. McKinley
Kamran M. Mirfa-khraie
Ali Mohamedi
Jennifer Morgan
Ihor P. Mykytyn
Frank Nargentino
Christopher S. Nicholas
Paul Nirenberg

Robert J. Palumbo
Rochelle Rachelson
Carmine A. Rizzo
Ruben Rodriguez
Mary Ellen R. Sacchetti
Dawn Sanflippo
Rooplah Shivdayal
Melissa L. Styron
Raymond J. Totillo
Linda Wong-DeJesus

**And the many specialty
contractors including:**

Stone and marble
Miller Druck Specialty
Contracting
Liberty Marble
A. Ottavino Corporation

Ornamental metals
Airflex Corporation
Coordinated Metals Corp.
Historical Arts & Castings
Raydeo Enterprise, Inc.

Steel/miscellaneous iron
F.M.B. Iron
G.C. Iron
U.S. Bridge

Electrical
L.K. Comstock

Mechanical
K.S.W. Mechanical
Penguin Mechanical

Masonry
M. O'Connor Contracting

Scaffolding
Universal Builders Supply

Plumbing
Greene Mechanical
Taggert Associates

*Construction Manager's
photographer*
Bernstein Associates

Sprinkler/fire protection
Rael Sprinkler
Sirina Fire Protection

Stone restoration
Remco

Terrazzo
D. Magnan Co.
Port Morris

Painting/plastering
Creative Finishes, Ltd.
Colletti Plastering
Hayles and Howle Co.
Strauss Painting, Inc.

Ceiling restoration
John Canning & Company
with the support of Felicity
Campbell, art conservator
EverGreene Painting Studios
(initial test)
Integrated Conservation Resources,
Inc. (initial conservation analysis)
Kinnari Silberman Restoration Inc.
(twenty foot patch)

Glass/storefront
Genetech
Tajima
W&W Glass

Clock synchronization
Kleinknecht Inc.

INDEX